Going Solo

Going Solo

Doing Videojournalism in the 21st Century

G. Stuart Smith

University of Missouri Press   Columbia and London

Copyright ©2011 by
The Curators of the University of Missouri
University of Missouri Press, Columbia, Missouri 65201
Printed and bound in the United States of America
All rights reserved
5 4 3 2 1   15 14 13 12 11

Cataloging-in-Publication data available from the Library of Congress
ISBN 978-0-8262-1923-7

♾™ This paper meets the requirements of the
American National Standard for Permanence of Paper
for Printed Library Materials, Z39.48, 1984.

Jacket design: Susan Ferber
Typesetting: Jennifer Cropp
Printing and binding: Integrated Book Technology, Inc.
Typefaces: Minion, OCRA, and Officina Sans

To everyone who has ever picked up a
camera to tell a story by themselves

Contents

Chapter 7

Chapter 8

Chapter 9

Preface

Some of the best stuff I've ever written for TV, I composed while looking through the viewfinder of a camera. Some of the best stuff I've ever written for TV, I composed after logging video shot by an excellent photographer. Some of the best—and most gratifying—TV stories I ever told, I never wrote a word. I just let the pictures, sound, and people tell their stories.

I began my news career in radio, but always enjoyed photography, using my 35mm camera to explore the visual creativity that my radio job didn't allow.

When I moved to TV, my first job—and probably best job I ever had—was as a one-man band, shooting 16mm film in a bureau where I determined what stories to cover and when to do them. Even while working primarily as a reporter, I kept a hand in the videography side, sometimes picking up a Betacam to shoot stories by myself.

Like most journalists, there have been many stories in my career that were not fun, just hustling to get accurate information and get it out quickly to the audience. But there have been many occasions when the storytelling has been fun and creative as well. Those happened when I worked by myself as a one-man band and when I worked with a photographer. I know there are times when working alone has drawbacks; dividing the work can be productive; collaborating can be inspiring. There also are times when working alone has been more productive and fulfilling than waiting around for a photographer to get one more angle or coming to loggerheads over whether to use a particular shot in editing the story.

I have won awards for both TV reporting and news videography. I have produced newscasts; I have worked in news management and I have produced two documentaries working mostly as a solo videojournalist. As a journalism educator I now have the luxury of time to study the industry. What I have witnessed is a trend toward more news operations utilizing what we used to call one-man bands and now call by a variety of names.

I know well the pros and cons of the arguments about one-man banding or solo videojournalism. I also know from experience what it takes to go solo, to produce a video news story on a deadline without the help of another person.

What I don't know, however, is exactly what to call the people who are at the heart of this growing phenomenon. One-man band is no longer in style, and there are now several titles that have been used to replace it. Depending on the corporate entity that employs them, they are called videojournalist, backpack journalist, digital journalist, or multimedia journalist.

What I have settled on is the term solo videojournalist. The word videojournalist is a combination, like the term photojournalist. Solo, obviously, implies someone who works alone, unlike a TV reporter and photographer team who work as a pair, but each is still, in his or her own right, a video journalist.

So, you will see the term solo videojournalist, VJ, or just plain videojournalist used throughout this book. It seems to be generic enough to cover the spectrum of companies that have adopted the concept in whatever nomenclature they use.

You will find while reading this book that VJs are making a difference in our news media. The concept truly has been born again to find a new life in television and online news media. What the genre lacks, however, is an instructional manual. There are many texts about reporting and volumes on videography. But, as far as I can tell, no single text has combined the skills into one that shows people how to master the unique requirements of each. *Going Solo: Doing Videojournalism in the 21st Century* attempts to do that.

Yet this book represents only a snapshot of the solo videojournalism genre in the early twenty-first century. I could not visit every newspaper, TV station, and Web operation that utilize VJs. While gathering information and writing this book, the field of solo videojournalism has been constantly evolving. Some of the things I first discovered no longer exist as they did before. I have made every effort to make sure that the book is as up-to-date as possible at the deadline.

One of the problems in doing this book in a timely way is that, as in all media jobs, people move on as better opportunities strike. So some of the people profiled no longer work at the organizations where I first met them. When I know of their departure, I have documented them either in the narrative or the endnotes.

Thanks to all who took time to help me do original research for the book. Those folks include Mike Sechrist, Steve Sabato, Melissa Penry, Jerry Barlar, Joe Gregory, and Matthew Zelkind at WKRN; Patti Dennis, Dan Weaver, and Heidi

McGuire at KUSA; and Dan Adams, formerly at KGTV. At newspaper Web operations, thanks to *washingtonpost.com*'s Tom Kennedy, Chet Rhodes, Christina Pino-Marina, and Ben de la Cruz; at HamptonRoads.TV, Chris Kouba, Patrick Buchanan, Brian Clark, Audrey Esther, Craig Kimberly, and Les Robinson; at the *Fort Myers News-Press,* Kate Marymont, Cindy McCurry-Ross, Mackenzie Warren, Christine Lee, Jessie Vega, Marc Beaudin, Mark H. Bickel, Amy Sowder, and Jackie Winchester. Thanks also to Roger Richards formerly of the *Norfolk Virginian-Pilot* and multimedia journalist Angela Grant.

Thanks also to Hofstra University's School of Communication, which provided some faculty grants to help offset some of my travel expenses for the research. Finally, a big thanks to Pam Deitrich for support and advice as the book advanced through so many stages.

Going Solo

Chapter 1

A Rose by Any Other Name

When Barack Obama delivered his inaugural speech on January 20, 2009, millions of people watched on traditional TV and cable news channels. Millions more tuned in from work on their computers. But they didn't choose news text services. They went online to *see* the speech streamed online, setting a record for people tuning into Internet Web sites to watch video.[1]

As President Obama delivered his speech, furloughs, downsizing, and resource sharing were the watchwords for many industries dealing with the deep recession. With technology advancing and more than two-thirds of Americans telling pollsters that traditional journalism sources are out of touch with what they want from news,[2] unlike past recessions, this downturn had long-lasting effects, permanently changing the ways news media companies gather and disseminate information to the public.

"The changes are going to be wrenching in the industry," says longtime magazine photojournalist and video convert Dirck Halstead.[3] The general manager of WMAQ, Chicago's NBC-owned TV station, Larry Wert, warned: "There is a major sea change happening in this industry, and we've got to be proactive."[4]

Many newspapers cut the staff of their Washington bureaus.[5] Even though U.S. troops were still stationed in the war zone, television networks slashed personnel covering Iraq.[6] To help remain competitive in international coverage, ABC News adopted a variation on the solo videojournalism (VJ) model, creating one-person digital journalists working from their own homes in seven foreign cities. The cost of all seven VJ offices was about the same as the fully staffed

1

Paris bureau, which closed.[7] The network added four digital journalists working in the United States in 2009.[8] CBS followed suit, hiring a VJ to cover Afghanistan in 2009.[9]

One-man bands, long a niche in the TV news business, began moving to a mainstream position as more stations cut two-person crews and adopted VJs to cut costs. The solo videojournalist not only reports and writes stories, but also shoots video and edits them.

Newspapers Relying on VJs, Too

VJs are playing a role not only in the traditional video news medium, television, but in formerly print-only organizations as well. As newspapers' circulation and revenue faced steep declines, some downplayed the printed product to concentrate on delivering news on the Web. As a result, video is becoming more of a dominant product across the Internet. Newspaper videojournalists and those with other multimedia skills are playing an increasingly important role in the business once dominated by ink and paper.

The Pew Research Center for the People & the Press reported 2008 was the first year that the Internet topped newspapers as a news source. In a survey in which respondents could select more than one choice, most people still got their national and international news from television (70 percent), but the Internet became number two at 40 percent, followed by newspapers at 35 percent. That continues a trend in which the Internet's share of the news audience tripled from 2001 while, at the same time, newspapers lost a quarter of their readers. And while TV news still seems to be king, television news saw a decline in viewers in the Pew survey as well.[10]

A Gallup poll confirms the disappointing numbers for most news media in 2008. Even in the hotly contested election year, the Gallup poll found the audience shrinking for all news media except cable TV news and the Internet. The poll's conclusion: "These data suggest the audience may still be there for most traditional news sources, underscoring the need for media organizations to find new ways to turn eyeballs into revenue. For many, this may require discovering creative ways to capitalize on the growing thirst for Internet news."[11]

Solo Videojournalists to the Rescue

In the face of those numbers, news managers increasingly are adopting solo videojournalists to remain competitive. At the NBC network flagship station, WNBC-TV in New York, managers revamped the news operation to launch a twenty-four-hour cable news channel that would rely on one-man bands.[12] WNBC's use of photographer-reporter combinations for its so-called content center is designed to make news coverage more efficient. "With that," says the station's general manager, Tom O'Brien, "we're going to see some benefits of productivity."[13]

At WMC-TV, which cut fifteen jobs in the economic downturn, news director Tracey Rogers has two one-man bands covering the outlying areas of the Memphis market. "All journalists need to have multiple skills in order to do their jobs," says Rogers.[14]

Gannett stations WUSA-TV in Washington and WTSP in St. Petersburg, Florida, reassigned some of its news and sports reporters to be multimedia journalists, who are expected to write, produce, shoot video, and cover live events for the Web site and broadcasts.[15]

A reporter working as his own photographer is not a new phenomenon. The TV news business used to call them one-man bands. Now, with so many women videographers, it's no longer a politically correct term. And others look down their noses at one-man bands as a small-market phenomenon. Plus, as TV stations and newspapers as well as other news organizations strive to find their niche in an increasingly competitive and downsized news and information market, more modern phrases are emerging to describe the work of those who are increasingly taking on the tasks of both reporting and shooting their own video. If one-man bands doesn't quite fit, what term does? Solo videojournalists? Multimedia journalists? Backpack journalists? Do Platypus, SoJo (solo journalist), MoJo (mobile journalist), APJ (all platform journalist), or digital correspondent aptly describe the functions?

As the video equipment continues to get lighter, cheaper, and easier to use, working as a one-man band, or VJ, is no longer a small-market TV phenomenon. KRON in San Francisco and WKRN in Nashville, both owned by Young Broadcasting, use solo videojournalists, or VJs, to cover stories. KGTV in San Diego calls its VJs digital correspondents; WUSA in Washington calls its reporter-photographers multimedia journalists and sister Gannett station, KUSA in Denver, uses the corporate moniker of backpack journalist (BPJ) for its one-person bands. Others using VJs by one name or another include the BBC, CNN, Associated Press Television (APTN), and some local cable news outfits such as New York 1 News and News 12 in the Bronx—not to mention dozens of small- and medium-market TV stations.

In fact, a 2010 survey by the Radio Television Digital News Association[16] and Hofstra University found that 81 percent of TV newsrooms utilize one-man bands in some way. The survey discovered that nearly 15 percent of the stations in markets one to twenty-five mostly use one-man bands and another 46 percent in those markets use them to varying degrees. Stations in smaller markets use VJs with even more frequency.[17]

"When I became news director, I became pretty frustrated with the number of people in the newsroom versus the number of people who actually leave the building to tell stories. I think all reporters should have some video capabilities," says Patti Dennis, the news director at the NBC-affiliate KUSA in Denver, who utilizes backpack journalists in her shop. "If we have one hundred journalists,

Small cameras have made it much easier for VJs
and fueled the trend to solo videojournalism.

say in our newsroom, and only thirty go out in the streets, something's wrong with the equation. We've got to get a few more story gatherers."[18]

WUSA and KUSA are owned by the Gannett Corporation, a media giant that owns both television stations and newspapers, including *USA Today*. The head of the company's TV operations, Dave Lougee, says the challenge is to get more stories for his audiences without sacrificing quality: "Are we a better newsgathering operation with 20 $50,000 cameras or 100 $7,000 HD cameras? We've got our newsrooms actively, intellectually engaged in how to define quality journalism in a digital age, and how to utilize the tools available to us to get there."[19]

Newspapers and Radio Adopting Solo Videojournalism

In this new age, now many radio stations are even requiring reporters to shoot video for their Web sites.[20]

Not to be left out in this convergent media age, newspapers are pioneering new ways of video storytelling in an uncharted terrain of online video. The Society of Professional Journalists (SPJ) monthly magazine, *Quill*, devoted a cover story and twelve pages to "Backpack Journalism," with tips for newspaper reporters who come face-to-face with audio and video recorders for the first time. In his overview article for that issue, a Nashville newspaper editor and then SPJ president, Clint Brewer, wrote, "Now, it appears there are three things certain in this life for journalists: death, taxes and video."[21]

At the *Plain Dealer* in Cleveland, the newspaper's online entity is trying to compete in a 24/7 news cycle instead of a single publication each day. That means video is a key to success. "We've got people who, a year ago, were still photographers, and now the majority of their time is spent doing videography," says *Plain Dealer* editor Susan Goldberg.[22] *Detroit Free Press* videographers produced a feature on singer Aretha Franklin, "40 Years of Respect," and ended up winning a News and Documentary Emmy, a traditional television news award.[23]

Many of those newspapers are adopting the solo videojournalist model to tell video stories on their Web sites. Many just call their reporter/photographers videojournalists, but Gannett has a corporate name for its reporters sent out with a combination still and video camera: MoJos, or mobile journalists. Some newspaper and magazine photographers who are turning to video have adopted the name Platypus, which derives from the animal's unusual ability to survive in two different universes, both land and water, just as a solo reporter-photographer has to survive and thrive in two elements.

The *Washington Post* and other papers have armed some veteran print reporters with video cameras. "We would buy the camera and give them to reporters to shoot still pictures, record voice, or shoot video," says James Brady, the former executive editor of *washingtonpost.com* who instituted the changes. "It's a triple-threat device. It adds a whole different dimension than you can get on the print side."[24]

At the *Wall Street Journal,* reporters are carrying video cameras to help publish twenty-five to thirty videos each day on the paper's Web site.[25] The paper's deputy managing editor, Alan Murray, says that the *Journal*'s reporters see and do a lot of interesting things. "And by putting video cameras in their hands, we have another way for them to tell their stories, another way for our users to experience what they're experiencing."[26]

As a result, newspapers are threatening the domain that used to belong exclusively to TV videographers. In the process, newspaper Web sites, with less emphasis on reporter narration, unconstrained by television's timed newscasts and a willingness to experiment with video techniques taboo on TV, are also redefining what videojournalism is all about.

Yet even solo videojournalists in the newspaper Web industry are not immune to layoffs. *Washingtonpost.com,* among others, have restructured their multimedia organizations and downsized a number of their videojournalists.[27]

Other newspapers experimented with various forms of videojournalism online, but have given up on the ventures. *HamptonRoadstv.com,* owned by the *Norfolk Virginian-Pilot,* started its own Web cast, *The Dot,* aimed at eighteen-to thirty-four-year-olds; it featured a fast-paced roundup of the day's news, with news packages from the Web site's solo videojournalists.[28] After some lay-offs, the remaining VJs are still doing packages, yet after a few years of the experiment, the *Virginian-Pilot* dropped *The Dot* from its line-up. "We're still kind of figuring it out, what the model is," says VJ Brian Clark.[29]

VJs Setting a Trend

Nevertheless, newspaper VJs have set a trend that will be hard to ignore in the future. A magazine writer, Kurt Andersen, profiling the surge in newspaper videojournalism indicated that TV needs to keep an eye on the usurpers: "I can easily imagine newspapers' Web-video portals becoming the TV-journalism destinations of choice for smart people—that is, in the twenty-first century, the dominant nineteenth-century journalistic institution, newspapers, might beat the dominant twentieth-century institution, TV, at the premium part of its own game."[30]

One case in point: The *Washington Post's* Web site "was commended for general excellence in video coverage online," in a Radio Television News Directors Association's Edward R. Murrow contest, and also has won Emmys and a Peabody, all awards normally associated with broadcasting, not newspapering.[31] The newspaper's VJs also have walked away with a substantial number of awards for video in the White House News Photographers Association, often beating their TV counterparts.[32]

Even smaller newspapers are getting into the VJ business: in Oshkosh, the *Northwestern* newspaper reporters are now heading out into the field with video cameras on their shoulders. A *Northwestern* news article gives management's pitch for the conversion: "Rest assured, video will only strengthen the newspaper's traditional role as a community watchdog. But it's guaranteed to give you a fresh, online reflection of life in your community, as you live it and it unfolds."[33]

Some newspapers are even requiring their photographers to use high definition video cameras instead of still cameras on assignment. All they have to do for a single image for the paper or Web site is grab a high-quality frame from the video.[34]

How It All Began

Solo video/multimedia/backpack/digital/journalists—one-man bands—who are producing news video for the twenty-first century have come a long way from those who pioneered the art. First there were the newsreel camera-

The Associated Press is one group that is using the VJ system to cover the news.

men who documented events worldwide for audiences on movie theaters' big screens. Following in their footsteps, television news crews in the mid-twentieth century began broadcasting their stories to much-smaller home screens.

"TV is the most difficult news medium to work in that has yet been invented," CBS News correspondent Charles Collingwood was quoted as saying in a 1968 book on television news. "It's mechanically more difficult, more cumbersome, it involves more people and uses more skills and puts more burdens on correspondents than either radio or the press."[35]

That book, *TV Covers the Action,* describes a network news operation as using three or four people in a crew. One was the correspondent or reporter, another the film cameraman, with a third person operating the sound recorder for the film. If needed, the crew added a fourth person to do the lighting.[36]

Getting everyone's ideas for how to handle the story became a crucial journalistic milestone: "All three must know how they are going to cover the action, must take into consideration the correspondent's own basic approach to the story and know what each can contribute. Then they must decide jointly how they are going to get it," the book's authors concluded.[37]

In the 1970s networks and stations phased out film coverage, which took a half hour or more to chemically process the film. Instead, stations adopted electronic news gathering (ENG). Those were electronic cameras and recorders that recorded moving images and sound on videotape, which gave news crews instantaneous access to images without developing. Even with the cumbersome arrangement of having the video camera attached to a three-quarter-inch videotape recorder by a cable, local stations cut the soundman out of the equation to simplify and make TV news gathering more cost efficient. The reporters concentrated on gathering information and interviews; photographers, with the camera on either a tripod or one shoulder and the recording deck, that some referred to as "boat anchors," on the other shoulder, managed to shoot video, get usable sound and do lighting set-ups if needed.

"The camera was powered by a battery belt that resembled weights that scuba divers wear," recalls Mickey Osterreicher, who shot with an RCA TK-76, an early ENG camera, at WKBW-TV in Buffalo. "An additional battery belt was needed to power a 250 volt Frezzolini light. It is amazing to think that with all of the connecting power and video cables not to mention mike cords that we were able to get anything shot. But we did."[38]

As cumbersome as that was, many got their start in television news working as one-man bands using that gear.

Later, Betacams mounted the video recorders on the back of the camera and scaled down the size and weight of the ENG equipment considerably. Networks usually dispatched a soundman along with a correspondent and Betacam videographer, but at local stations, two-person crews became the norm. Yet at many small-market stations, Betacams made working alone as a reporter-photographer far easier in this second generation of ENG.

One Person Getting Closer to the Story

Working with such equipment in the 1980s, Jon Alpert turned one-man banding into a TV news art form, using a *cinema vérité* style to get up close to people and do stories with angles few others were able to get. As a freelancer, Alpert sold many of his stories to NBC News, where he became a regular feature on the *Today Show*. Reporting and shooting in places that NBC crews could not or would not go, such as Cuba, China, or Vietnam, his reporting won several Emmy awards as well as a duPont-Columbia award.[39]

Alpert often injected his personality into his stories, which many critics decried. Yet a *Columbia Journalism Review* article in 1991 said, "Alpert hung around with his subjects long enough for them to let something human shine through the camera lens."[40]

The *Today Show* executive producer at the time, Steve Friedman, found Alpert's approach refreshing compared to the pieces aired by the traditional network news crews. "I thought, this is the kind of stuff that we can't get, because we can't spend that kind of time with people," said Friedman.[41]

Today Alpert has moved on to do long-form documentaries, usually with a crew, but his style of reporting, working one-on-one with subjects, gaining rapport where two-person crews can be a crowd, became a model for many solo videojournalists.

Solo Videojournalism Goes Mainstream and Online

As Alpert's run on the *Today Show* was ending, the miniaturization of video cameras, or camcorders, began and solo videojournalism as a movement started to take its first baby steps. Although it could also mean "video jockey" as in disc jockey, the term VJ as videojournalist first was used in Britain in 1994 as Channel One pioneered the art form.[42] About the same time, former CBS producer Michael Rosenblum became an advocate of reporter-photographers using Hi-8 cameras, getting up close and personal with people, spending more time on stories and developing quality videojournalism stories.

Rosenblum founded Video News International (VNI), working with about thirty people around the world armed with the small-format cameras. His target market was the networks' newsmagazine programs that allowed freelancers the time to develop long-form stories. Former *60 Minutes* producer David Turecamo used the VJ concept to develop, shoot, and edit a story on a week in the life of a small Haitian town. Working through VNI, Turecamo sold the story in July 1994 to ABC's *Nightline.* A producer for the program said she was delighted to get an in-depth piece that got "closer to the source of real people and real stories."[43]

At about the same time, as cable continued proliferating into American homes, news became a highly valued source of programming and began expanding. Time Warner's New York 1 News became one of the first twenty-four-hour local cable news channels, deploying mostly one-man bands in the heart of the nation's biggest media market. In a fifteenth anniversary salute to that groundbreaking effort, NY 1 News general manager Steve Paulus said in 2007, "We may not have a helicopter, but we can put more reporters on a story than anyone."[44]

Also in the 1990s, along came the Internet. At first the news media used it as a mere promotional tool, then found it was useful to transport news text and pictures across the planet. Soon, some enterprising souls figured out that video, too, could be a player on the World Wide Web.

The first ones to catch on to that phenomenon were still photojournalists. Dirck Halstead began training photojournalists to shoot video in conjunction with a National Press Photographers Association video workshop at the University of Oklahoma. "I decided that photojournalists really were the best people who were equipped to do this," Halstead says, "because they have the eye, they're used to carrying stuff. And so I started the Platypus workshops in March 1999."[45]

The first Platypus workshop attracted three Pulitzer prize-winning photojournalists. In the next months, the photojournalist-converts produced nine video segments for ABC's *Nightline,* "which is a staggering success," adds Halstead.[46]

Within a few years, not only newspapers were putting video on the Web with their solo videojournalists, but some major market TV station news operations also began adopting the VJ method as a way to stay competitive.

Top among them is KRON, a longtime fixture in the San Francisco TV market. Young Broadcasting beat out NBC in a bid for one of the most-watched TV stations in the city. In 1999 Young paid $823 million to the *San Francisco Chronicle,* which owned KRON. But NBC switched its network affiliation to another station in the market and left Young Broadcasting with an independent TV brand that had far less value to viewers. Consequently, Young has been struggling in programming—including its news—to make up for viewers and revenue it lost in the network switch.[47]

In 2005 KRON's managers sought to revitalize the news operation by converting reporters and photographers to solo videojournalists and hiring Michael Rosenblum to train them. Before the switch, the station had no more than a dozen two-person crews on the street. But Rosenblum said the five-week cross training would provide more stories by sending up to fifty VJs out covering stories.[48]

Not only did KRON cut costs by converting two-person crews to VJs, the station also saved money by using cheaper cameras and laptop editors instead of the standard Betacam equipment still in use at other stations.[49]

Some news critics called many of KRON's news stories amateurish, but the news director at the time, Chris Lee, stood by the venture that allowed the VJs to cover beats and do specialized reporting. "We're going to have three or four times the number of cameras on the street as any other TV station. That's going to allow us to invest in stories that don't pan out—but also go for stories that could pay off big," said Lee. "I firmly believe that we'll come out of this a far better station journalistically."[50]

Under the old system of two-person crew live shots, KRON reporter Mark Jones says his stories looked like many others "and I hated what I was putting on the air every single night." As a VJ, he began producing a franchise report "On the Move," about traffic and roads in the bay area. "I will shoot the story, I'm editing stories and feeding them from my home office over the internet to KRON on many occasions," he told a NORCAL RTNDA workshop on VJs a few months after the system started. "I'm having the most fun in broadcasting that I've had, I'd say, in at least a decade anyway."[51]

Three years after KRON began its VJ experiment, Young Broadcasting put the station up for sale as revenue continued to sag.[52] Yet for some of those VJs in the news trenches, it was an exciting place to be at a dramatic time in the business. VJ Jonathan Bloom told an interviewer, "You know the whole business is going to look like this and I'd rather be ahead of the curve instead of trying to struggle and catch up."[53]

For VJ guru Michael Rosenblum any setback is just a temporary delay in the transition to an inevitable outcome. "We're talking about a change in the basic economic construct of the television newsroom," he told an audience about the KRON VJ experiment. "We're not talking about one-man bands. We're talking about re-architecting the television news source content in a totally different way."[54]

Solo Videojournalist Timeline

1920	1930	1940	1950	1960	1970	1980	1990	2000	2010
Silent newsreels	TV news begins	ENG begins	Small videotape cameras developed	Internet news starts	KRON uses VJs
Sound added to newsreels					
		Jon Alpert on NBC		Small digital video cameras developed	VJ trend escalates on TV and
				ABC Nightline starts using VJ stories	newspaper websites

VJ timeline

Solo Videojournalists as the Wave of the Future

One news consultant admits the trend of downsizing and asking people to multitask will continue and those fighting it will just have to accept the new paradigm. "We are an industry that has to stop whining and move forward," says Jerry Gumbert, the president and CEO of AR&D Consulting.[55] Yet Gumbert says cutting costs alone is not the best long-term strategy for news media companies. "We tell them to reengineer the newsroom to operate in a world with new revenue realities," he says.[56]

A major daily newspaper taking steps to survive in that climate is on the frontlines competing with television in using video to cover local news. The *Detroit Free Press* announced it would scale back home delivery of the paper to three days a week to concentrate on its Internet product. The news release from the *Free Press* said the paper was putting extra emphasis on multimedia and up-to-the-minute news and "looking to develop our broadcast capabilities ... to offer video reports and broadcast news" on the Web.[57]

CNN, which began its online service in 1995 and now finds it a highly profitable venture rated as the number-one news Web site, doesn't plan to rest on its laurels. "Fear of change can send you to a very conservative place," says K. C. Estenson, CNN.com's general manager. "We want to redefine the news experience."[58]

Looking beyond the existing structure of news organizations, as camera gear continues getting cheaper and lighter, solo videojournalists could become key content providers as media companies work past the downsizing to become leaner news providers for niche target audiences. Some start-up Web news operations targeting niche audiences, such as NeighborhoodMedia.com already have VJs supplying some of their content. Much of the audience will continue moving away from their traditional TV sets, newspapers, and magazines to find news where they want it, when they want it.

As technologies change, to survive, all the news media will have to be hunter-gatherers, following the audience to whatever platform people choose to read, watch, or view. Much of the world already is seeking alternatives to the traditional news media. Media executive Mark Effron writes, "for those who grew up in what they thought were 'the good old days,' it's time to get over it. We have to stay relevant and interesting and on the edge of technology and society, and we must always remember: At some not-too-distant point in the future, these are going to be the good old days."[59]

Even with all the changes and enhancements to technology, however, news managers still will need to emphasize serving the needs of their audience. Professional media watcher Diane Mermigas says that to continue to be profitable, media companies need to find better business models to unlock the potential of the technology. The key, she writes, still will be to produce quality that people want. "Tech-empowered consumers appear to be more interested in the end result than in which screen it comes on. They prefer interactivity rather than passivity."[60]

One value of the Web is that the user controls the experience instead of the news manager or producer. As a result, TV news organizations may need to rethink whether their standard packages will work online; they could give users more options for short video segments that they can click in and out of as well as the narrated versions of VJ packages.[61] In addition, as newspapers and TV news organizations already have discovered, publishing news on the Web will continue to be the primary breaking-news outlet, putting it online before their traditional newscasts go on the air or the newspaper hits the doorstep.

Many employees will find themselves challenged to change and keep up with this media dynamic. Dave Delozier was a photographer at KUSA when managers called on him to convert to a backpack journalist. "If you're looking for reasons for it to not work, it won't work," he says. But as the fifty-four-year-old looked toward the end of his career, he was committed to making it work. "The change is going to come. Either wait for a wave to you knock you over or jump on that surfboard and ride it," says Delozier.[62]

As the VJ model—in whatever iteration it is called—is becoming increasingly accepted, the concept has gone from small-market TV to mainstream for all types of news organizations. ABC's Mike Lee may have set the trend for network coverage. The ABC Web site extols the virtues of this solo videojournalist: "Lee set out to the far-flung corners of the world, with a small DV camera, a laptop computer, a satellite phone, and a mandate to look for unusual stories that show the audience the rich diversity of life in cultures and societies often overlooked in day-to-day news coverage."[63]

Now with VJs going mainstream, they are even being recognized with their own award. The National Press Photographers Association (NPPA) gave its first Solo Video Journalist award in 2007. It went to a backpack journalist, Dan Weaver, at KUSA in Denver.

So, whatever we call them, VJs, BPJs, MoJos, multimedia journalists, Platypus, or digital correspondents: a one-man band by any other name would smell as sweet. The fact is, this method of news gathering for TV, newspapers, and other Web-related media outlets is on the rise and here to stay.

Discussion and VJ Exercise

1. Find out what news organizations in your community are using solo videojournalists. Talk to news managers there about why they adopted VJs, how they are using them, and how well it is working. What title do local organizations use for its VJs? Why do they call them that instead of one of the other titles associated with solo videojournalism?

2. Look at stories on the Web or on TV and try to analyze whether they were produced by a crew or by a VJ. What techniques used in the story might be tips to whether it was produced solo or by more than one person?

3. Discuss exactly what costs the VJ method can save a news organization. Are there any expenses that working alone might have over a two-person crew?

4. There are a number of names associated with the position of a solo videojournalist. Why are there so many? What name seems to best describe the work that they do?

Chapter 1 Focus
"The Rosenblum Model"

Michael Rosenblum is practically synonymous with the term VJ. He has been pushing the concept of solo videojournalists since small, lightweight cameras became practical in the late 1980s and early 1990s. Television stations and newspapers have hired the former CBS News producer's company to train reporters to shoot and edit video and photographers to report, write, and announce their stories.

Rosenblum blogs about solo videojournalism; he speaks about it at professional conferences; he is a lightning rod for the controversy surrounding solo videojournalism.

The so-called Rosenblum model utilizes a solo videojournalist instead of a two-person crew to cover stories. Working with a lightweight, small camera, this model allows a VJ to develop a rapport with sources that a two-person crew might not be able to develop. The Rosenblum model eschews a reporter standup as well as a live shot that seems to focus more on the reporter than the story, which would be more of the one-man band style of reporting, according to Rosenblum. Often a station will use the Rosenblum-style VJ to cover features, beat reports, or sidebars of breaking stories.

Michael Rosenblum, speaking at a San Francisco debate on VJs, has been one of the main proponents of the movement.

Below is a compendium of comments Rosenblum has made about the topic at various conferences:

"We make crappy television, not because we're bad, but because the technology ties our hands. This liberates people to make a much better television.[1]

"In a newspaper, they have people fighting to get stories. That's what makes newspapers really powerful and dynamic. At a newspaper as a journalist, you can go out and say, 'I think there's a story here, I want to try it.' In a New York newsroom you do that and they give you a crew and you come back at the end of the day and say to your news director, 'You know what? As a journalist there wasn't really a story there.' You're fired. But now it's just you and your camera. So sometimes you go out and get a story and sometimes there's not a story.[2]

"Now for the first time we are in the business of making television in your hands. You have a vision like Mark [Mark Jones, a KRON VJ] has a vision. He's been given the tools, he understands how to use them. He goes and manufactures on tape what's in his head. And that's where television is going to go. The economics of this makes it absolutely, positively irresistible. This is going to happen.[3]

"As the audience gets more and more fractionalized, smaller and smaller, this becomes economically the only way to produce product in this thing. So I think there's a certain inevitability to this and there will be a much wider range of ways to produce for television than there is presently.[4]

"In certain smaller stations this will be used to cut costs. In all candor, I had a conversation with Sinclair [a chain of TV stations], they were very blunt with me about their interest in cutting costs and I walked away from the table because of my reputation; I don't want this to be known as a cost cutting measure."[5]

Rosenblum came to his conclusion that solo videojournalists are a practical way to cover stories and a better way to be a journalist when he was at CBS News.

"I quit in 1988, which is a long time ago, because what I thought most of what we were doing was lies and crap in all honesty. For those of you in the network business, you know the producer goes out, they do all the work, the on-air, over-paid correspondent shows up at the last minute, says 'Who we talkin' to?', they get shot into the piece and it goes on the air."[6]

When Rosenblum quit CBS, he got a small S-VHS camera and went to a refugee camp to live with and profile a Palestinian family.

"And even though I was a producer at network, I had never shot anything before, because we all know you're not allowed to touch a piece of the equipment, which is kind of an act of insanity.[7]

"Most significantly, being and living with the family 24/7 with the camera, gave me a certain intimacy that a typical reporter couldn't have . . . Journalism requires time; it requires a personal relationship. So, these little cameras, more than anything else, let me spend time.[8]

"The other thing I discover is any idiot can do this. Because the thing about video is, it's immediate; you know what it looks like. So you shoot something, you look at it right away: you don't have to spend four years at NYU film school to know that's a bad shot, that's a good shot."[9]

Rosenblum started selling his video stories to NBC, ABC, and PBS.

Rosenblum also began his own news service and started training others to work as solo videojournalists.

"If you use the little cameras like one-man banding, and you say 'Put it on a tripod, do a standup, replicate exactly what you do with the big cameras, you don't understand the potential of what the gear can do. It's completely different.[10]

"There's a fundamental difference between videojournalists and one-man bands. One-man band, let's face it, is a cheap way of trying to imitate what the larger stations do. You get this one guy, you give him the camera, you give him the tripod, he drags this stuff around, he puts it on a tripod, he takes a mic flag, he does a standup. At the end of the day you have some crappy looking, maybe cobbled together stuff, that tend to approach what the better stations do. These little tiny cameras give us the opportunity to completely change the grammar, the way the thing looks. These little bitty cameras . . . is not one-man banding. It's the creation of videojournalism as a kind of communicative journalistic tool, just like photojournalism was a communicative journalistic tool.[11]

"This is videojournalism, which is journalism done with a small camera. So we encourage the reporter to use the camera as a kind of a notebook, to do interviews, to take notes. We generally don't do any standups. It doesn't really work this way to make standups. It tends to be much more intimate; it tends to be much more, almost cinemagraphic in terms of its construction.[12]

"Newspapers have a distance to go. And I think that we can find historically, that when new technologies come along, there's almost a 20- or 30-year gap between the arrival of the technology and its application."[13]

As a result of people working solo, Rosenblum says VJs can turn out more stories than typical two-person crews.

"Each VJ should ostensibly do two or three pieces a week. It gives them an enormous amount of time to go and find the story, do the reporting and really craft something. Now that means the news agenda changes. In the typical newsroom, the first thing we do is open up the newspaper. And the reason we open up the newspaper is because we only got about six or eight crews to fill the news hole, so we can't have a crew come back and go, 'No story there, that didn't really work out.' So, in effect, when we do local news we end up re-treading what's in the newspaper already. Everybody in town has already read it; by the time it gets on the air it's 24 to 36 hours old. When you have a cadre of 50 reporters with cameras, you can have freedom to fail, which is important to journalism. It means you can say, 'I have a story I want to do. I'm not sure if it's real or not.' I can say, 'Stacy, go take the camera, go find out, maybe it works, maybe it doesn't work.' You can't take that kind of risk in a conventional newsroom. That's really the difference.[14]

"The best protection you can give to union members is to teach them this skill set. If you can shoot it and you can cut, you are employable for the next hundred years. If these two people come and apply for a job in two years and this lady on the left says 'I can shoot, I can cut, I can edit, I got a laptop, I make this every day,' and this lady says 'I need a cameraman, I need a soundman, I need a producer, I need an editor,' who's going to get hired? The best job protection you can get now is to learn the skill set and understand how to do this. It makes your employment airtight.[15]

"It cuts the cost of production by about 50%. It quadruples the number of people in the field. It improves the journalism. We found much more adaptation of this in Europe than we have in the United States. The United States tends to be very slow and also ironically Americans are quite technophobic. We find the Scandinavians, the Germans and the Dutch and maybe even the English, I'm not sure, adapt and embrace new technologies much, much faster than Americans do. Americans are really frightened of change."[16]

Chapter 2

VJ Is Like a Cussword

As shown in chapter 1, using VJs may be a cost-effective way of covering more news than using two-person crews. Yet news media operations converting their reporters and/or photographers to VJs have found themselves mired in controversy. Employees hired for one position sometimes are reluctant to take on the duties of two.

Solo videojournalism guru Michael Rosenblum has been at the forefront of the crusade extolling the virtues of VJs. The former CBS producer has consulted with several TV stations and news organizations overseas converting to the system. "When television was invented," says Rosenblum, "it didn't come with an instruction manual; God did not descend from Sinai and cast in stone: thou shalt have a cameraman, thou shalt have a soundman, thou shalt have a producer. Those functions grew out of because the cameras, they weighed a ton and you needed someone to carry them around to do it."[1]

Solo videojournalists with reporting, researching, shooting, writing, editing, and Web skills will find themselves valued employees doing the work that several people in the past would have done. At KXTV in Sacramento, anchor Dale Schornack started shooting and editing many of his own franchise "Good People" stories in 2007. "If I can go out and shoot my own story, and do it well," he writes in his station blog, "it frees up a News10 photographer to go to other assignments with or without a reporter. More news content from the same number of people."[2]

"If you have that skill set, you set yourself apart," says WKRN-TV's Matthew Zelkind, who took over as news director of the Nashville ABC affiliate about two years after the station converted reporters and photographers to VJs. "You make yourself a valued employee."[3]

Those who have been entrenched in other positions are going to have to be flexible, learn new skills to survive in the rapidly changing industry. Big-market sports reporters are not immune to the trend. At KMOV in St. Louis, some of the sports reporters have surrendered to the inevitable. "No one here in sports at Channel 4 is happy about it," says KMOV sports director Steve Savard of using a backpack journalist. "But layoffs now in the business are pretty much the norm. I think we're entering the lean-and-mean phase in this business."[4]

NBC correspondent Kerry Sanders says he has worked as a solo videojournalist "only out of the country (due to union rules) and only in cases where a crew could not come along for political reasons." He cites Cuba in the early 1990s, when the Communist country was not allowing journalists in, but did allow tourists. "So with camera in hand, I entered as a tourist and reported several stories on how the economy was faring absent the support once provided by the Soviet Union." Sanders doesn't like the idea of working alone on TV stories, but for the Cuba story he concludes: "Worked great for what it was."[5]

How Does VJ Quality Compare?

When the National Press Photographers Association awarded its first Solo Video Journalist award in 2007 judges' comments were underwhelming. "The winners in this emerging category cobbled together stories that exhibited poise and sophistication," writes judge Jay Korff. "The quality of the remaining entries dropped off significantly."[6]

"Does doing it by yourself in the field and in the edit bay lead to the best storytelling?" asks Joel Eagle. "The results say no. The top three stories were solid and well done. After the winners, the drop off was significant."[7]

"This was a tough category to know where to set the bar," adds NPPA judge Regina McCombs. "A number of truly great photojournalists have essentially been one-man-bands, but most of those who entered in this were young journalists getting started. We ended up with an assortment of spot news, features and general news that's a bit of apples and oranges, on top of the fact that none of us are thrilled with the idea of the proliferation of vjs in the first place."[8]

Deborah Potter, a former CNN and CBS correspondent who now is the executive director of NewsLab, is concerned about one-man bands creeping from small-market to larger stations. She is not opposed to people working as VJs if they are "adept" at it, but adds, "One-man banding is nothing you aspire to. You aspire to put that behind you."[9] She admits that being a VJ can help one's storytelling skills improve, but the major drawback is one person trying to accomplish two journalistic skills at the same time; it puts a lot of pressure on people and is hard to do.[10]

Yet Potter admits in one article: "There are situations where working alone is the only viable option." She adds: "But the best television photography is the product of good thinking, not just point a camera in the right direction and pushing the button. And getting crisp, clear natural sound often requires a second set of hands to hold the microphone."[11]

Others are more blunt: "If you go to any message board in the photography world, the two words 'VJ' is like a cussword," says NPPA board member Brad Ingram.[12]

The Heart of the Controversy

Some of the drawbacks to doing both sides as a reporter and videographer are obvious. One person can't be in two places at the same time. If a two-person crew is covering an event a reporter can talk to a source and get information while the photographer is setting up, getting video or breaking down the camera. VJs "can't while shooting the fire, sidle over to a firefighter you've run into on previous stories and find out while chatting that the arson squad has been called in," David Page wrote in a blog responding to the rise of VJs. "I'm sure there are cases in which one man band is fine. But, bottom line, in most cases it is a solution that steps back, not forward in fulfilling a journalism organization's compact with its audience."[13]

Canadian VJ Nicole Lampa says it can be exhausting working solo. "It's never easy, for example, to knock on the door of a murdered boy's home to ask his mother for a comment or a photograph," she writes, "but imagine having to do

Two-person crews allow journalists to focus on either the reporting or the videography.

that while asking the grieving woman to wait as you set up the tripod. You simply cannot do this gracefully, and it can be an emotionally draining experience for the videojournalist, too."[14]

A veteran reporter at Washington's WUSA-TV decided to leave the station rather than convert to working as a backpack journalist. "It takes a lot of time to shoot and edit and write and prepare a story," said Gary Reals, "and if you have one person doing all that, something has to give."[15]

Reals told a Washington-area publication that he worried that the substance of the reporting would decline as the station made its transition to BPJs: "If you're involved in the shooting then subsequently the editing, you can't be thinking too much about the journalistic aspect of gathering additional information," he said.[16]

Yet some who work as VJs disagree that the quality of the work suffers when the jobs are combined. Formerly just a reporter, Eric Mansfield converted to a backpack journalist at WKYC-TV in Cleveland in 2008. He notes in his blog that going solo may be an economic necessity, but does not hinder quality reporting. "I know that one month of using the camera and editing my own material," he writes, "has already made me a better journalist."[17]

And in St. Petersburg, Florida, WTSP-TV backpack journalist Janie Porter agrees, writing: "it is rewarding because I know that I did it all by myself." Yet Porter adds that when working alone, "you have to be smarter about how you use your time."[18]

With newspapers sending out reporters with video cameras, now even they could be the targets of critics who complain that it divides journalistic skills and compromises the product. The online editor for the *Indianapolis Star,* John Strauss, took a whole multimedia bag of tools to cover the state fair and ended up with thirty-two blog entries, twenty-six photos, and five videos over a ten-day stretch. He concluded, "Without a doubt, the better way to generate that amount of content would be to use at least two people, with duties tailored to their specific skills."[19]

VJs Need Total Involvement in the Story

"Your senses have to be totally involved. And your intellect has to be totally involved,"[20] says Dirck Halstead, a former still photographer for *Life* and *Time* magazines who turned to producing video stories in the 1990s. Yet Halstead, who founded Platypus, a group dedicated to training still photographers in the art of video storytelling, defends the solo videojournalist model. "I would argue it's much better for the simple reason that it is totally under the control of one person," he says. "Everything is that photographer's concept."[21]

As newspapers rush to put video online, the technical expectations for VJs seem to be lower than for their TV counterparts. "We don't expect them to be

Capra right out of the box," says *Washington Post* foreign editor Keith Richburg.[22]

As a result, most of the debate over quality is still centered in TV newsrooms. Stuart Watson, a reporter at WCNC-TV in Charlotte, admits he can shoot video. "But if you look at my videography or editing, you realize pretty quickly there's a reason God made real editors and videographers. And if you listen to some of the writing and voice work on the VJ pieces you'll find there's a reason God made anchors and reporters."[23]

When Washington's WUSA-TV set out to convert its newsroom to multimedia journalists, the station's general manager saw it as a way to stay competitive in an increasingly fragmented media market. "We believe strongly that [this change] will raise both the quality and quantity of the product," said Allan Horlick.[24]

NBC correspondent Kerry Sanders disagrees that the push to VJs is driven by quality. He says the conversion is strictly economic and taking its toll on journalism. "The reality is those who want the widespread use of them [VJs] are looking at the dollar and cents costs and they see savings. I see a different cost, lost opportunities to best tell a story."[25]

Some VJs disagree that their work is inferior to two-person teams. "My work as a photographer is expected to be as strong as the photographers whose sole focus is on shooting and editing," says Justin Quesinberry, who worked as a backpack journalist at WFMY-TV in Greensboro, North Carolina. "My work as a reporter is expected to be as strong as the reporters whose sole focus is on reporting."[26]

One of journalism's top prizes went to a foreign correspondent who began working on the award-winning program as a solo videojournalist. In 2008 Richard Engel won a duPont-Columbia Award for his MSNBC documentary, "War Zone Diary." "I started filming it initially because I didn't have much other choice," says Engel. "I didn't have a camera crew; I was in Baghdad. I wanted to document what I was seeing. And at a certain stage, I decided I'll just keep a video journal partly because it was easier. I didn't have to think as much, I could just turn the camera on myself and talk." Besides his solo video diary, Engel supplemented "War Zone Diary" with material he gathered when he later started working for NBC News.[27] Engel also won a Medill Medal of Courage, which is awarded for "moral, ethical or physical courage in pursuit of a story." He is the first broadcast journalist to win the honor.[28]

Another VJ, freelancer Mara Schiavocampo, won an honorable mention in the Society of Environmental Journalists Outstanding Television category in 2007 for a story about an oil spill in the Mediterranean Sea. The judges remarked: "She brought to light an environmental disaster most had never heard about and was able to show the effects on local people."[29]

One of the toughest tasks for VJs is paying attention to what an interviewee is saying while also making sure the camera is framed and operating correctly.

As for her work as a VJ, Schiavocampo says, "I think in the next five, 10 years this is really going to revolutionize television, because why would a news organization pay for a sound guy, a camera guy and a correspondent to go somewhere when they can pay one person?"[30] NBC News apparently learned that lesson as well; the network hired Schiavocampo as a digital journalist in October 2007 to produce stories as a VJ for both *NBC Nightly News* and the organization's Web site.[31]

Even though former CBS and CNN correspondent Deborah Potter says the best TV photography is the product of "good thinking," that does not necessarily exclude people who report and shoot by themselves. Indeed, many a TV photographer has griped at the excessive primping and cosmetology of their reporter teammate as they prepare to be on camera. And critics say far too often TV stories seem to be about the reporter more than about the story's subject.

VJs may automatically overcome some of that. They are invested in the story as both the reporter and videographer; as a result, they may put more emphasis on the journalism and the storytelling—the total package—more than a two-person crew would. "Most reporters think it's all about them," says Tampa's

WFLA-TV anchor Keith Cate. "But if you've ever been a one-man band and actually done the photographer's job—when you've had to huff and puff with that camera—you have respect for it. It gives you greater perspective."[32]

Solo Videojournalism as a Stepping-stone

Countless TV reporters and photographers got their start in the business as VJs or one-man bands. Most have moved on to specialize in either one area or the other as well as advance up the media ladder to better-paying jobs and more recognition. But even if they were eager to leave the physically demanding experience behind them, many who worked as VJs seemed to come away with skills that make them better at their craft.

Many shared the lessons—both the positives and negatives—they learned by working on their own.

"I was so grateful for the experience of being the one-man band and having to go out and shoot my own B roll and shoot my own interview," said former *Entertainment Tonight* correspondent Jann Carl. "Shooting your own standup was difficult, but it can be done. I still wear that little secret badge of honor that I know how to do all that."[33]

"With time deadlines and with limited movement on stand-ups it's hard to be as creative as you want to be. I also found it very taxing on warm summer days . . . it takes its toll after a while," says Andy Douglas, an anchor in Memphis. "I don't think I was a good writer when I was a one man band, but I think when I made the jump from one man band to reporter I focused more on the writing and that in turn made me a better writer and a better overall journalist." Yet on the positive side, "You also really appreciate having a photographer later in your career."[34]

Another former one-man band had the opposite experience: "I became a much better broadcast journalist by shooting and editing," says former news director and ABC producer Bruce Cramer. "I could visualize the story—start to finish. I knew what shots I needed to help me tell the story. So yes I became a better writer—writing to my video—letting the words and pictures work together."[35]

Former St. Louis TV reporter Brenda Madden Kimberlin agrees that an earlier job working as both reporter and photographer helped her later in her TV news career: "It definitely made me a better writer and story-teller . . . And I learned how to spot/develop video options for so-called 'non-visual' stories . . . a skill that really helped me when I moved into city reporting, which involves a lot of crime scene tape, etc."[36]

NBC correspondent Michelle Kosinski says she sometimes misses her days as a one-man band bureau chief in Charlotte, North Carolina. "I just found the experience to be fun, satisfying and empowering," she says. "It helped my writing, producing and shooting all at the same time."[37]

"My experience as a one-man-band had taught me what I wanted from these photographers, some of whom were obviously better than others," writes former Nashville and St. Louis TV reporter Aaron Mermelstein. "I knew what they, the camera, the lens and the film could do. Sometimes I honked them off asking for shots they would not have necessarily made, but it made my stories better and often made them better shooters."[38]

"Shooting one man bands did force me to learn to think about all aspects of the story, pictures, sound and the written story. I believe that experience paid off later when I became a news director," says former Savannah, Georgia, news director Mike Sullivan. "Having 'done it all,' I could relate to all the different jobs in the newsroom."[39]

One horror story about covering a parade featuring Miss America comes from Nancy Pasternak, who worked as a one-person band in Biloxi, Mississippi: "I was about 112 pounds carrying the ¾ deck and camera. I was walking along shooting and the whole crowd was like 'Wow, look at Miss America, look at Miss America' . . . when it suddenly shifted to 'Look, the newsgirl fell . . . the little girl fell.' I had tripped over [a] construction horse. Equipment flying, legs bleeding . . . the whole crowd ignored Miss America and came to my rescue."

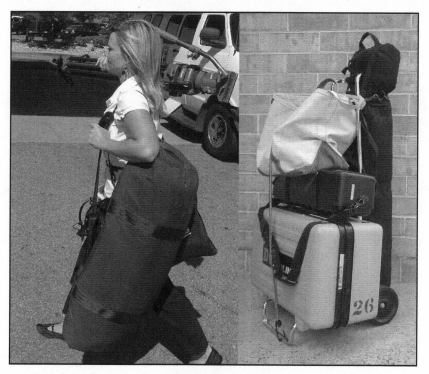

Solo videojournalists have to do it all themselves, including carrying their own gear. A small luggage cart can ease the burden.

Yet overall, Pasternak says working solo was a positive experience as she moved to a larger market in St. Louis. "It sure made me appreciate photographers and editors—and I'm proud to say—if something major happened—I can still edit with the best of them and probably shoot fairly well."[40]

A Liberating Experience—or Overworked?

It may be tough working as a VJ, but no one says the experience killed them and most admit they became better video storytellers to boot. As a result, more stations and newspapers are opting to choose solo videojournalists to help them deliver their news product. Some cynics complain that the switch is just a way for bottom-line oriented news businesses to cut costs: it's obvious; one person covering a story costs less in salary and benefits. Yet news managers admit that the VJ model is not designed to cover each and every story that crosses the assignment desk. The big story of the day and breaking news stories often are assigned to two-person crews by TV stations. Newspaper Web VJs also cover some breaking stories, but mostly seem relegated to covering evergreen stories where one person can easily manage the deadlines of both writing the story and editing the video.

At an RTNDA debate over the use of VJs at KRON in San Francisco, one reporter-to-VJ-convert, Mark Jones, says he was skeptical of the concept at first, but he was also tired of doing an "endless succession of live shots" that looked "exactly alike." He sees his reporting differently as a VJ: "This is not just a way to cut costs," Jones said. "I think it can be a way to make TV news much more compelling, much more interesting and much more fun to do."[41]

At that same conference, a reporter at a competing station, Wayne Freedman of KGO-TV, called the reporting by the photographers-turned-VJs "kind of medium market to tell you the truth. The pacing was off; the writing was off; the transitions were off. The structure was wrong; the story didn't flow." Freedman concluded: "If someone else out there in the field and someone else out there in the edit room [had been] working on the thing that was a little bit too long, it might have been a better story."[42]

Yet a few years later Freedman, who has a reputation as one of the country's premiere feature reporters, evolved into working part of his time as a VJ at KGO. "Love my photographers, love working with them," said Freedman at that 2005 NORCAL RTNDA conference, "but what I would miss most is the collaborative element, the idea that having to edit it alone, when working on the thing, yeah this works, no this doesn't . . . and when you have one person working alone, where does that go?"[43]

Five years later, however, Freedman says as a solo videojournalist, he discovered that VJing is more appropriate for long-term "hold for release" type of stories than breaking news. Despite one academic study that shows solo videojournalism in TV news is less likely to "foster innovation,"[44] Freedman says at the ABC owned-and-operated KGO-TV having VJs allows the station in tough economic times to cover some things that it wouldn't have been able to do with two-person crews. So, he concludes, having VJs has enhanced enterprise reporting, "It has raised the standard of what we do."[45]

As a former TV news photographer, Freedman has adapted well to that part of the VJ's job. He's "not even close" to being as good as the best photographers he's worked with, says Freedman, but now working alone as a VJ gives him greater flexibility: "I can do as much as I want with a story without the desk telling me I need your camera in 30 minutes." As a result, Freedman now says he often can't wait to shoot his long-form stories by himself.[46]

Other VJs also find working alone liberating: "There isn't any discussion or arguing over what shot to use. I never feel like the timing is off or that the edit looks bad," writes Janie Porter. "Because it's just my vision of the story, and not a compromise between two people . . . I often feel my backpack journalism packages bring the viewer more quickly to the essence of the story."[47]

One drawback to working alone, however, is the inherent issue of having more safety while working in pairs. In dangerous situations, it may not be safe to send a VJ out to cover the story. Even two-person crews have been attacked or harassed from time to time. Yet a reporter and photographer working together can watch each other's back whereas one set of eyes and ears may not provide adequate protection.

One-on-One Can Mean More Rapport

In the end if it has compelling content, VJs with small cameras can make a story work. NBC VJ Schiavocampo finds that she can do more working alone and carrying less equipment. "I get a lot of access because one woman with a camera is easily ignored, easily missed," she says.[48] Several VJs find they can establish a better rapport, or intimacy, with their interviewees by working alone.

A former VJ at *washingtonpost.com* sums up the advantages: "This video journalism vision of single authorship throughout the process will get you some really interesting results," says Travis Fox, who is now a freelance VJ. "And as the technology gets simpler, if more individuals shoot and cut video—like they create writing—you are going to get a lot more interesting styles, and a lot richer body of work as a whole."[49]

The best niche for VJs seems to be situations where two people with a big camera and live truck just seem to change the nature of the story, where one person with a small camera can build rapport with a subject and tell a detailed visual account of that person's perspective. "There's an intimacy to this [kind of storytelling] that is much more like the intimacy of radio," says ABC *Nightline*'s former executive producer, Tom Bettag, who championed a number of pieces by freelance VJs. "The difference is wading in with four people and a ton of equipment versus one person with a microphone. It changes the environment."[50]

David Snider did a VJ story for *Nightline* about Ellen Bomer, who lost her eyesight in the embassy bombing in Nairobi, Kenya, in 1998. She was able to regain some of that sight through rehabilitation. "She had already turned down several other major networks; she wasn't interested in being the fuel for the daily-news fire," Snider writes. "She trusted that she wouldn't be portrayed as a victim, but as a normal person who is having an extraordinary experience."[51]

Snider says the key to getting the story was being able to work quietly and unobtrusively with a DV camera, like a "fly-on-the-wall." "As a videojournalist, it was enormously satisfying to witness Ellen's delight in her new vision."[52]

Discussion and VJ Exercise

1. Find a current-event topic, then write a one-page summary about how you would approach doing a video story differently working as a VJ versus being in a two-person crew.
2. List what strengths you have as a potential solo videojournalist. Also list areas that you need to work on to improve your skills as a VJ.
3. Work with another VJ-in-training to stage a debate about this topic: "Resolved—working as a solo videojournalist makes it easier to produce more engaging stories about subjects."
4. Develop a story pitch that you will do as a solo videojournalist. List ways that you will approach the story to overcome the limitations of working alone as described in this chapter.

Chapter 2 Focus
A VJ Documentary Experience

"Ha, ha, it's gonna be a jammin' start," the Milkman laughed standing next to the mast on Four Sheets to the Wind.

"Go for it!" someone shouts next in the natural sound sequence.

The sloop's starboard winch whirrs into action as the crew approaches the starting line for the first yacht race from the United States to Cuba since Fidel Castro took power.

As several other sailboats converge on the start, the captain's wife cries out, "Let it out big time!"

"Main out! Main out!" yells Captain Bill Sheets as the crew hustles to harness every ounce of wind power.

Bill's wife screams at another boat just yards across the shimmering Gulf of Mexico: "No spinnakers at the start!"

That video sequence appears near the beginning of *A Bridge to Cuba,* a documentary I did as a one-man band. The project actually started as a story for the NBC TV affiliate in Fort Myers, Florida. That five-part series in 1994 showed how Americans and Cubans were building friendships across the sea despite the obstacles thrown in their way by the two governments. One key segment showed how Carolyne Sheets had bonded with a five-year-old boy whose father had become a *balsero,* a refugee who risked his life on a raft to reach America, a few months before.

The series also opened viewers' eyes to the hardships Cubans face just to survive each day. With my small S-VHS-C video camera, I followed two American sailors into old Havana, where a woman invited us into her home. She opened her refrigerator to show what the family had to eat that night: five potatoes and a jug of water.

Two years later I sailed back to Cuba with a High-8 video camera to start turning the five-part series into a documentary for public television. Instead of the adventure of the sailing trip, this time I focused more on the friendship the Americans and Cubans were building, especially how Bill Sheets and his wife, Carolyne, were struggling to decide whether to smuggle the refugee's wife and her then seven-year-old son into Florida to join her husband. In 1998 I sailed again to Cuba on *Four Sheets to the Wind* as the Sheets continued giving aid to what they started to call their "Cuban family."

Two years after that I took my video camera to capture the Sheets greeting the father, mother, and son as they were reunited in Miami. It was a happy ending to a six-year-long saga—a fitting ending to a story that, because of the expense and space restraints, would not have been told if I had to rely on a traditional TV reporter-photographer team to help me tell it.

When this story first started in 1994, I was a reporter, though one who got his first TV job as a one-man band and one who occasionally picked up a video camera when space or other circumstances did not permit me to work in a traditional two-person crew. When I saw the potential groundbreaking story of sailing in the first yacht race to Cuba since 1959, I asked Captain Sheets if I could accompany him on his thirty-six-foot sloop. Two factors helped me become an embedded member of the crew: (1) there was just me; I didn't need a second person to shoot video; (2) I wasn't just dead weight with a camera; I had sailing skills that could help get *Four Sheets to the Wind* to Marina Hemingway and back to Florida.

The author has produced two documentaries working as a solo videojournalist.

Sailing to Cuba three times was an adventure. Making *A Bridge to Cuba* was a satisfying journalistic experience because it was a dramatic story that no one had ever told before. But if I couldn't have worked as both the reporter and videographer, the story never would have been made public.

"Definitely looks like refugees of some kind," Captain Sheets says peering through his binoculars. The crew of Four Sheets to the Wind *is making a brisk return voyage from their first trip to Havana. Less than thirty miles from Key West they spot a small boat loaded with seven Cuban refugees bobbing in the shark-infested waters.*

"Cuba, Cuba," one of the refugees shouts out to the Americans. Captain Sheets orders the crew to haul in the sails and motor over to the tiny boat to give them food and water.

"I can't believe this," Carolyne Sheets says, tears streaming from her eyes. "They lost people in the water."

After witnessing the hardship and poverty facing the Cuban people, discovering and helping the refugees releases a flood of emotions in the Four Sheets *crew. I point my video camera at the "Milkman," a hard drinking, stocky construction worker who has tears flowing down his cheeks. "I can't believe we're doing this. After just coming to Cuba and seeing them. These people are the bravest people on our side of the world, I know that," he finishes with a loud sniff.*

The Americans call the Coast Guard and hover near the Cubans for two hours until a patrol boat comes and takes them to shore. These Cubans are lucky: they will be allowed to stay in America; a few months later, because of the thousands of Cubans streaming into Florida, the government changes its policy to return any Cuban refugees found at sea.

That was a memorable scene witnessed by countless viewers in both the original five-part local series and later in the public TV documentary. Whatever you want to call my role: one-man band, solo videojournalist, or backpack journalist, it would have been a story left untold if I had not been able to be both the reporter and videographer.

Now many more such stories may see the light of day on either television or the Internet. With smaller, cheaper cameras, digital laptop editing, and an economic revolution in the media, those participating in the rebirth of videojournalism are able to tell more stories cheaper and faster and leave fewer important stories untold.

Chapter 3

Preparing to Shoot the VJ Story

As critics already have pointed out in this book, solo videojournalism requires multiple skills that not everyone can master. Yet hundreds of VJs have performed the multiple tasks of reporting, interviewing, shooting, editing and, yes, time management that it takes to do the job well.

"When I was covering hurricanes, I was working both as a backpack journalist and as a photographer for a reporter," says KUSA-TV's Dan Weaver. "So I would usually edit their stories, edit my stories, shoot their live shot, switch and get in front of the camera and do my live shot and then we've got an hour to redo it all: redo their package, redo my thing and us both get out there for the next show. And it was crazy."[1]

Most texts separate the skills required to be a videojournalist into tasks of either reporting or videography. This book, however, looks at the combination of skills that it takes to work successfully as a VJ. This chapter tackles the preliminary phases of the news-gathering process: coming up with a good story, tips on finding good characters for a story and making sure video equipment is working properly before arriving on the scene to discover a crucial malfunction that will delay or ruin the story.

The VJ's Clock Never Stops

Later chapters will have more tips on doing the story on the scene as both the reporter and photographer as well as tips on writing or organizing the story. Each will have some time-management tips specific to the task, since deadlines are always looming and the clock never stops at any point in the process.

Dan Weaver works part of his time as a VJ at
KUSA and says meeting deadlines can be hectic.

"That was probably one of the first lessons that I had to learn, was good time management," says Heidi McGuire, a backpack journalist at KUSA-TV in Denver. "If I'm going to take an hour and a half to write this package, then I'm only going to leave myself forty-five minutes to edit it. You end up screwing yourself," she laughs.[2]

"It's true that one person can do the work of four, but no matter how you dice it," says St. Petersburg's WTSP-TV anchor and backpack journalist Janie Porter, "it's going to take one person longer. That's why time management is so important."[3]

So, the first time-management tip is always keep an eye on the clock. Set interim deadlines to help you meet the final deadline for the story. If you have a story to air on the six o'clock news, get back to the office by four p.m. to log the video, write the story, and do an error-free edit. That means you may have to scrap an interview with a subject who can't meet until five p.m. Instead, get the information over the phone and utilize that in your copy or standup.

"I think setting deadlines for yourself is good," says Brian Clark, a VJ at the *Norfolk Virginian-Pilot.* "It's all too easy to sit in front of this computer until midnight because I don't like something and I want to change it. Or I can narrow the focus; I want the thing to be a minute thirty and get it in on time."[4]

If you have a longer-term assignment that is not due for a few weeks or months, set your own deadlines for writing and editing much earlier than the final due date. The extra time will give you flexibility in meeting any unforeseen challenges.

As you get faster at using your camera, more adept at writing a well-focused story in a hurry, and know all the bells and whistles on your nonlinear editor, then you might feel comfortable trying to squeeze in that five p.m. interview and just insert the video on your timeline. Until then, give yourself plenty of time to beat the clock.

Find a Story That Lends Itself to Being Told on Video

Before a VJ can shoot a thing, the reporter side of the equation must come up with a story idea and information that makes it all relevant to the target audience. Sometimes stories just land in journalists' laps. A variety of spot news events take place or a tipster calls the news desk with a legitimate idea. Most of the time, however, journalists have to dig up story ideas. Chapter 11 deals with techniques to help VJs become enterprising reporters for the long term, yet every day reporters will be challenged to find stories that are compelling and meaningful to their audience.

Every community has lots of meetings, ceremonies, and events that a group of people will be interested in reading about or seeing covered in video. Many news organizations now are covering such hyper-local events to post on their Web sites. Yet those may not be stories that will garner large audiences. The ultimate goal is to find stories that will generate enough interest for *everyone* in a community to watch.

Even those stories can be divided into breaking news versus those that have a more "evergreen" shelf life. The former will have a short life span; reporters and editors will need to update them frequently as the story evolves. The latter category could live on a media outlet's Web site for months or years. Either category may—or may not—have compelling video elements to tell the story. A savvy VJ, along with his or her editors, will figure out a way to find the best multimedia elements possible for each story as it comes along.

If the story has few visual elements, it may call for text and graphics to make the best presentation for a Web site, or just a copy story for TV. Or it might demand an audio slideshow for the Internet. The VJ's skills could also be put to use to cover an event just to get sound bites and video for a newscast or the online product. A multimedia-ready VJ should be able to do all of the stories listed above.

But the highest and best use of a skillful VJ will be to produce a narrated package for a television newscast, a mini-documentary for a newspaper or magazine Web site or a natural sound package for either. Both the TV and Web genres require the same elements: well-produced action video with good natural sound that brings viewers to the scene and compels them to watch; people who have interesting stories to tell or can explain complex and intriguing issues in their own words; conflict, controversy, or a feature element that drives the story and keeps the audience glued to the screen to see how it all plays out.

Whether it's a breaking news story, a multilayered feature or an in-depth piece, the story should have some nugget ingrained in it that will make the audience care enough to watch.

Before heading out to the story, writing a one-sentence pitch can help focus on the most important story elements and keep the VJ on track to gather video, natural sound, and interviews—the raw materials—that will help the audience care about the story when the fieldwork is finished.

Find Compelling Characters

Once the VJ and the editors have agreed on a story, one of the hardest parts is finding good characters to build the story around. This is more of a reporting than shooting skill. But your alter ego photographer will benefit from the hard work it takes to find—and sometimes persuade—interesting people to become part of your story.

"The reporting part to me is still more important than the photography part of it," says Dan Adams, a former VJ at Sacramento's KXTV. "It's more important to be a reporter than it is to be a photographer."[5]

Facts are important, but it will be the people, not the facts, that your audience will relate to and remember. The people should be more than just sources for facts. Focusing on one person's experience can be a window that illuminates a larger issue, a way to personalize an abstract concept.

First, think of the work you will turn out as a story, not just a factual report about an issue or event with sound bites and video. Then think of all the novels you have ever read or movies you have seen: each has interesting, often compelling characters with dreams, foibles, and obstacles to overcome as a continuing plot in the story. Real people have stories to tell as well; their lives often are epic dramas. The VJ's job is to find an element of those lives that are newsworthy or will make a compelling feature that can be told in a minute and a half—or sometimes in a longer format—video.

Second, think again about those novels or movies. In the cast of characters there usually are two main characters: a hero/protagonist and a villain/antagonist are in conflict over something. You can borrow that model to tell a story that will grab viewers' attention. Many stories in journalism are about conflict; there is someone doing something that other people don't like. In those set of circumstances, often someone will stand out as trying to do the right thing or as attempting to overcome a seemingly insurmountable obstacle.

That could be the hero of the story, someone who can help you find the story's focus.

In this simple storytelling model then, those who are standing in the way of the hero might be a villain.

Look for Nuances in the Characters and Issues

Of course, since journalists are trying to illuminate the truth, not create a fictional work, there will be many shades of gray: the character who appears to be trying to do the right thing may have motives that are not so pure; the person standing in the way of that may have the rule of law on his side. There may be multiple sides to the story, each with valid points in their favor. Yet the conflict between these sides is essential in good storytelling. The people who represent those sides are critical in helping viewers understand and relate to the issues involved.

Even in spot news coverage, there may be opportunities to develop people in your stories as heroes or villains. Is there a person who called 911 and saved a family from burning to death? Sounds like a legitimate hero. Mother Nature also provides plenty of opportunities to personify nonhuman events as characters. The tornado ripping through a town at three a.m. while people were sleeping, Hurricane So-and-So aiming at the heart of the city, or oil washing up on a pristine beach all could be portrayed as a story's unspoken villains.

Most of the time, however, videojournalists are not thrust into a breaking-news situation. To develop a compelling story, the VJ often will need to spend adequate time on the phone finding not only facts and background information, but also interesting people. The reporter may luck into finding interesting characters on the first call. Or it may take a dozen calls to find a person who has the personality that will stand out on camera, is intricately involved in the issue being covered, and is available by the deadline for the story.

When he worked on long-form video stories for *washingtonpost.com,* VJ Travis Fox says he often interviewed people on background without a camera, sizing them up to find the right character for his stories. "It's kind of a casting process," Fox writes. "In some ways, it's two processes: the journalism and the video production."[6]

Besides just focusing on the main characters in the story, you should also try to find a variety of voices with multiple perspectives; at the very least, you should provide balance for controversial issues. That does not mean that for every interview for Side A you need an interview for Side B. It might be that some interviews are so strong and compelling that one interview is enough for that side of the story. You might need two or three interviews to balance that one strong interview—or to show that there are quite a number of people on one side versus those on the other. You also might need multiple interviews to show the nuances of the issue: one person might see merits with three issues on

Brian Clark says VJs should set self-imposed deadlines
to avoid spending endless hours working on a story.

Side A, but agrees with Side B because one point in the conflict is overwhelm-
ingly for that side. Other interviewees might also weigh in with totally different
perspectives from Sides C, D, or E.

Another thing to be aware of when setting up interviews or approaching
people in the field to do an interview: if appropriate to the story, you should
include a diverse array of ethnicities who can add different insights to the piece.
You don't have to use each and every interview you shoot, but you should have
a variety of interviewees and perspectives to choose from to make the story as
strong as possible.

Once you find the right combination of characters, much of the story will
fall into place, including opportunities for interesting b-roll, or video, of your
characters. See chapter 5, "Get Closer to Your Subject" for more information on
integrating characters into your video.

Check Out Your Equipment before the Assignment

"There's nothing worse than showing up somewhere and not having a light
or not having a battery or not having a tape," says VJ Brian Clark. "If you have
the right equipment and check the equipment properly then that's the first step
in having a good story."[7]

If the camera won't roll, the microphone batteries are dead, the car's gas tank is on empty, it may mean you miss getting video for the story. That means you don't get the story at all.

Check out all the equipment ahead of time to make sure you don't get left behind.

The checklist should include the following:

1. Turn on the camera. Make sure each camera battery has adequate power. Test the sound levels on the camera and the headphones. Make sure the audio cables work well without a hum or crackle. Check the wireless microphone as well and make sure the batteries are good. Have a backup supply of batteries for the camera and wireless, too. Roll the camera's record function. Is the tape recording? Is the card capturing? Play it back to be sure. Check the other camera functions such as iris controls, shutter speed, white balance, zoom, and any automatic features that may be needed.
2. Set up the tripod. Make sure it provides a steady platform. If it wobbles, repair the parts to make it secure again.
3. Check the lighting equipment. Are any bulbs burned out? Is a light stand missing a screw? Replace parts now before you need them in the field.
4. Make sure you have extra tapes or cards to record the story.

Multimedia journalist Tracy Boyer failed to test a new video camera before taking it to Honduras to do a story on malnutrition programs. "Low and behold, the audio feedback on my camera was somehow broken," she writes, "so I couldn't listen to the incoming audio while it was recording. Even worse, I couldn't change the frequency settings on the mics (I know it's easy to do in the menu settings, but it didn't work for some reason on these . . .) so my first two interviews were recorded at an almost inaudible level. After raising the levels in Final Cut and removing the hum in Audacity, it still wasn't perfect."[8]

Make Your Mistakes in Private

Another tip may be self-evident, but practice, practice, practice. Unless you pick up a camera, use it over and over and learn from your mistakes, you won't get better. Ron Sylvester, a newspaper reporter in Wichita, decided he wanted to be multimedia ready in his reporting. So he learned how to gather and use audio and video. "But it does take time," he writes. "And patience. And a willingness to stumble, which is hard for those of us comfortable with our hard-earned professional competence."[9]

Former TV news director Jill Geisler agrees that managers making employees convert from other positions need to give them time to practice the new skills. Now a media educator at Poynter Institute, Geisler writes: "If adults learn a new skill, but don't practice it right away, the learning fades. Only when a sufficient number of people adopt the new technologies and ways of working, can a culture really change."[10]

There are a wide variety of techniques to shooting a quality video story. Take one and practice it until you master it, until it becomes second nature. Then move on to other skills and practice each one until you master it. Soon you will have a litany of videography skills you can use when you need them.

Practice setting up the camera and your shooting skills before heading out on a story; make your rookie mistakes in private so that when you are working in front of an interviewee or in public, you will seem polished and professional.

Discussion and VJ Exercise

1. Given your level of skills as a VJ, what interim deadlines should you set for yourself if you had to have a fully produced package in six hours?
2. Write a story pitch for a target audience for your medium. The pitch should include a one-sentence statement that focuses on why this is a good story for that audience. Include how you will personalize the story around a main character, other people you will interview to help flesh out different perspectives, and what video you will shoot and what natural sound will be good to pursue for the story.
3. Take a story from a newspaper, TV newscast, or Web site. Make a list of ten sources you would interview to follow up on that story. Does your list of interviewees provide balance to any controversial issue involved? Is the list of interviewees diverse? Which interviewees would make a good "hero" or "villain" in the story model described in this chapter? Are the descriptions "hero" and villain" too simple or are there nuances in their positions that can work either way?
4. Make your own personal checklist of gear and other items you should take on your VJ shoot. Save the list and check off each item as you prepare for your next shoot.
5. Prepare a gear bag to show your colleagues. What things do you use when you are shooting that others may not use. How do those items make the shoot easier or more productive for you? If they don't make it easier or more productive, do you need them in your gear bag?

Chapter 3 Focus
Freedom, *Freedom*

Brian Clark is a solo videojournalist at the *Norfolk Virginian-Pilot*. Before that he worked five years as a TV reporter-photographer in Oregon. This is from an interview with Clark by the author.[1]

Q. How is it working as a solo videojournalist?

"I think whenever you're a one-man band, you have that freedom to shoot something, write something, put it together and it's yours; you own it. You can't blame a bad story on someone else.

"When I'm out in the field, you're shooting through the viewfinder and you're kind of writing the story as you're shooting it. It's kind of an intuitive thing, you know. The more you do it, the more it becomes instinctual-like.

"I think all too often people overshoot things. They'll come back and look at their footage and they'll be overwhelmed. Okay, I have all this stuff, what do I do with it?

"I think it's important to narrow your focus. Have kind of an idea of what the story should look like. You should have an idea of what you want so when you come back, you're not going to edit yourself into a corner, you're not going to write yourself into a corner. And since you already know what you have anyway, you're not going to write yourself into a corner.

"I miss like bouncing things off people. It's kind of like when you and your buddy go out to a bar. It's always nice to bounce things off of somebody who has a stake in it."

The Difference in Working Online Compared to TV

"I don't think there's one kind of stylistic template that we would use since we have more freedom than we would on television. On television you were told from day one you can't use music. Well, we have liberty to do that if it enhances the pieces.

"The deadlines are looser online than for a TV newscast. As a TV one-man band, there was little time after the morning meeting to develop a story and never time to be really creative since you had to have a story ready by 4:30 to get ready for a live shot. There is more opportunity to be creative in this format, with an unstructured deadline. There's no formulaic template to get done by 4:30.

"If I want to add more nat/snd there's nothing stopping me from doing that. Plus, producers want variations on the same story for different newscasts. You're being pulled in so many different directions.

"When I was in television, I really liked what I did, but I didn't really like the system.

"All too often in television news, you come to that point . . . in your career, people ask, what are you going to do? Are you going to be a reporter or are you going to be a photographer? And I didn't know, I didn't want to give up the camera; I didn't want to give up the content."

A former TV VJ, Brian Clark now likes the freedom
from time constraints that online videojournalism offers.

Chapter 4

Shoot with Your Eyes and Ears

After the bombing of the federal building in Oklahoma City, the Associated Press distributed a photo of a fireman carrying a baby injured in the attack. The infant's bloodied head is nestled against the fireman's right shoulder, her battered legs hang over his other arm. The fireman looks down despairingly at the limp, battered body as he rushes her to triage. Baby Baylee later died from her injuries; the photographer, Charles Porter, won a Pulitzer Prize for the shot.

Virtually everyone who sees the picture gets a sinking feeling, a sadness that brings back the shock and horror of that day. The picture has an impact on every person who views it.

No journalist wants to be thrust into a situation as horrific as the Oklahoma City bombing, yet that photographer did his job well, bringing the reality of that day home. It is a memorable snapshot of an infamous day, a piece of work that can't be thrust aside without feeling something about the victims of the tragedy.

Seek Shots That Have Impact

That is what videojournalists should strive to do in each of their stories as well. Every story should seek to have an impact on viewers—not just something that is sad, but information, images, and sound that will evoke a response or a feeling from viewers after the story is over. It could be a tearful response, but it could just as well be a happy and joyful feeling if that is what the story warrants.

The point is that VJs should make their stories memorable instead of making their viewers feel that they wasted their time watching meaningless video and information. To have that kind of impact, the reporter side of the equation must seek characters and information that bring the story to life, the videographer side must look for ways to keep the story visually appealing and stimulating.

The effort to create a story that has impact should be easier for VJs than it was to snap the picture of Baby Baylee. Think about it: Porter's shot was just one frame, less than a second in time. VJs have thirty frames per second of video, so when they tell a minute-and-a-half story, they have 2,700 opportunities to make their stories memorable with individual pictures. Each of those split-second frames has a new chance to have an impact on the audience.

Sounds easy, right?

Not so fast.

The danger is that novice VJs especially will have the wrong kind of impact on the audience—the kind of impact where people will be talking about how bad the sound is, how fuzzy the pictures were, or how the video is so dark that they couldn't see anything.

To get shots with impact, VJs often need to seek perspectives that people normally don't see while standing or sitting.

So, how does a VJ achieve the desired impact in which people will be talking about the feelings left by the story instead of the unwatchable video? Every VJ must correctly perform the techniques of videography. That means mastering the production values of clear sound, steady shots, focused subject matter, good composition, and correct exposure.

Dirck Halstead, the award-winning photojournalist-turned-videojournalist, says discipline and story planning are the keys to becoming a good VJ. He believes still photographers often make the best videojournalist converts. Yet he says they have to learn to approach a story differently. "Still photography is a linear form and it's about reacting emotionally to stimulus and capturing an image," says the Platypus trainer. "Video on the other hand is totally intellectual. Video, it's not your heart, it's your brain, because everything must be planned."[1]

Yet people from reporting backgrounds learn to master the production techniques to be successful solo videojournalists as well. Backpack journalist Janie Porter says that working alone requires being resourceful: "Use those sometimes annoying, curious bystanders to your advantage. Instead of shooing them away, enlist their help in recruiting interviews, getting directions, etc."[2]

If there were a checklist of things to do as a VJ, the reporting side of the equation could put the list in any order: D, B, A, C or B, A, C, D. The reporter can jot down a sentence for a story before doing an interview; she can look up file tape before making a call to a source—or she can do it just the opposite and it wouldn't make a difference.

But when it comes to shooting video, it's more of a science. The VJ has to follow a checklist to get the production values just right: A, B, C, D:

A. You have to white balance before you roll tape.
B. You have to plug in the microphone before checking the audio levels.
C. You have to zoom in to get a good focus.
D. You have to put the camera on the tripod to make sure you get steady shots.

If you don't follow the right sequence or don't do them correctly, you're going to mess up something.

The result will be that you will have video that is unusable—or if you decide to use it anyway, it could be so distracting that people will be noticing the poor quality instead of what you want them to pay attention to: the story.

Use Video to Transmit an Experience

Print journalists are good at delivering new facts, figures, and analyses in their stories. But even the best narrative-writing, ink-in-their veins reporters can't fully develop the human element, the raw emotion, the experience and reality that audio and video can display in two-dimensional color.

In short, a well-told video story not only delivers new information, it also brings home the experience of being on the scene to viewers. You are asking people to spend time viewing your work, so it needs to be valuable enough to spend their time on you. If you consistently deliver a story with new information and an experience people will remember, perhaps feel something about and talk about with their friends afterward, your stories will have greater value and give viewers a reason to watch your work.

Consistently doing stories that have impact is extremely hard work. But producing stories with creative words, pictures, and sound makes it possible.

It is a cliché, but it is true: a picture is worth a thousand words. Video with sound is worth 10,000 words. The rasp in the throat of a cancer survivor, the cheers of the crowd when a Little Leaguer hits a game-winning home run, the roar of a forest fire as it rages toward a subdivision: these are all pictures and *sounds* of scenes that even well-written prose convey faintly. It is the sound and the video combined that transmit the experience of seeing people, places, and events as realistically as possible.

Sound Is a Major Piece of the Story Puzzle

The first video task of a VJ is to work to get good sound in the field. "Bad audio can really ruin a good video story," writes the *New York Times*'s Ann Derry.[3]

At every step in the process the reporter in the VJ has to think about what sound and video she needs to tell her story. What sound bites are necessary from experts to break new ground? What bites from eyewitnesses or victims will add background and perspective? What opportunities are there for natural sound to help move the story forward?

As the photographer, the VJ must decide what video can best visualize the story's concepts and at the same time pay attention to the aural information coming at her from all sides of the story scene. Shooting to get adequate natural sound breaks will be key to giving the audience time to digest the information from the sound bites and narration.

"I kind of use those natural sound breaks the same way I use the interview material, because that goes a long way towards telling the story," says multimedia reporter Angela Grant, who specializes in telling her video stories without narration.[4]

That concept seems to be foreign to many who are turning to videojournalism as a new career. Newspaper still photographers who are picking up video cameras for the first time find it difficult to think about getting and using sound to tell their stories.

Chuck Fadely, a veteran photojournalist at the *Miami Herald* with more than twenty years of experience, was surprised how much sound played a role in his video stories: "I'm a bright guy," he says. "I'm a technology geek, and it is still very hard. It is a completely different way of thinking, to structure a video."[5]

Fort Myers News-Press photographer Marc Beaudin routinely does natural sound videos for the paper's Web site. Even though he took a TV production course at a community college long before he began shooting video professionally, changing from still photography to video required him to learn new techniques and skills. "The audio is really important. Really important," he says. "And that's one thing I think I was failing continuously beginning with this camera."[6]

For VJs attempting to tell their stories without narration, one key is to be sure to have an uninterrupted flow of audio. Reuters staff photographer Lucy Nicholson did not have much experience producing video stories, but was assigned to do one on a Times Square musician who calls himself the Naked Cowboy. Nicholson says she had to learn quickly how to develop videography skills instead of relying on her photojournalism skills. "The 2 most obvious mistakes I kept making in the beginning were: (a) not using a tripod with video, and (b) not asking questions which required the interviewee to respond with a full sentence in audio interviews," she says.[7]

To make sure the quality of the audio is good, the videographer side of the VJ must wear headphones. Even when there is something wrong, the audio meter on the camera will register a hum or other distortion just as it will clean audio. The only way to make sure you are getting clean sound is to monitor it through your headphones; if it is not clean, then analyze where the problem is and correct it to ensure you do get good sound. It also is wise to shoot with two active microphones in case one malfunctions.

If the on-camera, or shotgun, microphone is not adequate to pick up good sound of a subject from your location, then move the camera closer so you can get adequate sound. Better still, utilize a wireless microphone to get sound from people or objects from a distance. Without that, you may want to string an audio cable to the source of the sound and attach a lavaliere mic or position another microphone near the subject.

Shoot Natural Sound, not Noise

When shooting your story, recognize the difference between natural sound and noise. Natural sound, which emanates from the subjects you are shooting for your package, is one of the building blocks for your story.

Noise is a distraction.

If, for example, you are doing a story about rising milk prices and are shooting video of dairy cows from a fence along a highway, you may be getting more noise than natural sound. You could end up with what psychologists call cognitive dissonance. Your pictures for the story may be cows grazing peacefully on the grass; you might be lucky enough to get a close-up of a cow mooing. Yet if a parade of cars and semitrucks is barreling down the highway directly behind your camera, all you are going to pick up on the microphone is noise of belching diesel engines, blaring horns, and tires thumping over potholes. Viewers will see one thing and hear another. Using the traffic noise as sound underneath the video of the cows will be noise, a distraction from the story that will confuse your viewers.

Do everything you can to eliminate the noise and collect true natural sound for your story. Wear headphones, block extraneous noise with your body, get permission to go on the farmer's field to get the video and sound of the cattle close up. Work hard to get meaningful natural sound that will enhance the story instead of using noise that transmits a different experience than the one you want.

Wearing headphones helps ensure that VJs such as Heidi McGuire get useable sound and not just noise when shooting their video.

Sometimes you will even want to punch the camera's roll button just to pick up some sound you can use. If you haven't steadied-up the camera just yet, or you can't get a good shot for some other reason, you can cover the sound later with other video you have shot. But to maintain ethical standards, if you do use sound that way, make sure the video is from the same time and place you recorded the sound.

Shoot with Your Ears

Since sound is such a rich storytelling component, also be ready to move to where the sounds of the scene tell you to go. You can always edit out bad shots, but if you miss that crucial piece of sound to help tell the story, then you have missed an opportunity to transmit the experience and illuminate the audience.

The key is to shoot with your ears.

Anyone who has ever picked up a shoulder-mounted video camera knows the photographer has a 180-degree arc that is blind. The videographer can see in front through the viewfinder and to the left side with peripheral vision. But the camera blocks the right side view and no photographer has eyes in the back of his head. So, one's ears become the key to *seeing* what is happening on those blind sides. While you are rolling video, if it *sounds* as if something more important is happening behind you or to the side, turn around and get it. What you are hearing may make a better story than what you are already shooting.

The VJ should also anticipate where the action of the event is going and be there in plenty of time to capture the best sound and video. Don't be blindsided by an unexpected opportunity that you could not shoot because you failed to anticipate it. That may mean closely observing the scene or it may mean asking some questions of participants or organizers so that you are fully aware of the sequence of events that will take place.

When Shooting, Listen Like a Reporter

Day by day, practicing the craft of solo videojournalism will make each skill seem easier to accomplish.

For reporters, gathering facts and interviewing may seem natural. For still photographers, the lighting and composition may come more easily than it does for those who have never picked up a camera. Yet either can master the techniques of videography.

The key to being a successful VJ is to always keep the story in mind. Work to get good sound and video in the field so that you have a variety of pieces to construct a meaningful, compelling story when you return from the shoot. So, when shooting, *act like a photographer,* do all the necessary things to get the technical stuff on the camera right, but *think and listen like a reporter.* Don't let golden opportunities for better sound and video for your story pass you by.

Discussion and VJ Exercise

1. Watch a package from a local TV or network newscast and analyze how the reporter uses sound in the story. How much narration is there compared to sound bites and natural sound breaks? How could the reporter and/or photographer better utilize sound in the story?

2. Look at a newspaper's Web site and look at the video stories produced for it. Some may be what are considered mini-documentaries with no narration and a lot of sound bites and natural sound. Is it a well-told story? How does the story hold together without a reporter's narration to give it context?

3. Choose an event in your community to cover with a video camera. Interview at least three people and shoot video with natural sound. Your goal is to shoot the video with your ears, to get at least six natural sound breaks for a 1:30 package. Have a colleague critique your raw video with careful attention to natural sound that you can use to build the story.

4. Log the video you shot in Item #3. Transcribe the sound bites with the time codes at the beginning, interim points in the bite, and a final time code. Do the same with your natural sound. Log the description of the natural sound as well as the video, with the in and out time codes. Log your raw video with explicit descriptions and specific times of how long the shots last.

Chapter 4 Focus
Converting a Reporter to a VJ

"Joe Gregory to South Paducah!" the voice calls over the intercom on the lower level at the WKRN studios in Nashville. The summons comes from Melissa Penry, a WKRN VJ with an infectious laugh, who named the area around her cubicle South Paducah because she and another nearby worker both hail from Kentucky.[1]

It's late afternoon and after several swigs of Dr Pepper while editing her video, Penry is ready for her story to face scrutiny from the station's chief photographer.

Once a radio reporter, Penry came to WKRN in 1985. Twenty years later when the ABC affiliate made the decision to convert its news reporters and photographers to VJs, she went along for the ride.

Melissa Penry converted to being a VJ after
working several years as a reporter at WKRN.

All that shooting and editing stuff was new to her when she went through
the training with the rest of the staff. Penry admits it took her awhile to get the
hang of editing. "When I first started, it took me a lot longer to edit than it does
now," she says. The first video story she edited at her desk on the Pinnacle system took half a day. But eighteen months later she says it may take only thirty
minutes or sometimes less when she has to "crash" a story on deadline.

Earlier in the day Penry worked the phones to set up her story. "Do you know
if the other students have permission to be on television?" Penry asks on the telephone. She is heading out to a local high school where a female student has just
been accepted into West Point. "This is a true VJ piece because it's about one person," Penry says while making the twenty-minute drive to the school.

When she pulls into the visitors' parking spot, she walks to the rear of the car
where her gear is stored; she stuffs a wireless microphone, cables, and extra battery into a waist pack, pulls her HDV camera out of its case, and hefts a tripod
and heads for the school office to sign in.

While waiting for a student escort, Penry chats with a secretary as if she has
known her for years. Penry in a pink jacket, dark slacks, and graying hair has a
favorite aunt-like quality that just seems to put people at ease. When the escort
arrives, Penry gathers her gear and treks to the school's back forty where a por-
table classroom houses the JROTC unit.

Despite her earlier comments about this being a good, single-source VJ story, Penry interviews not only the student appointed to the military academy, but also her army instructor and several other JROTC students. After hooking her subjects up to a wireless microphone and checking her audio meter and head-phones to make sure she's getting good sound, just like a veteran videographer, she interviews different people so they are facing opposite ways on camera: first she stands on the left side of the camera so the appointee faces that direction; for the next interview, she flips the camera viewfinder so she can stand on the right side of the tripod and have the subject facing that way.

Most of her interview subjects are taller than Penry, so she raises the tripod several inches above her head for the camera to be at eye level with her inter-viewees.

When finished with the interviews, she shoots a few wide shots from the tri-pod, but in the cramped quarters, she removes the camera from the tripod and hand-holds it to get most of her video. "I probably overshoot," she says, "just to make sure I have something good." And since she's working alone, focusing primarily on the shooting, a notepad rarely emerges. "I can't walk around with a notepad. All of my notes have to be mental or on tape."

Taped to Penry's viewfinder is a small strip of paper. Typed on it are the words "Align-Frame-Sequence." These are terms she learned for video se-quencing when she went through the VJ training. A few years later, she doesn't

It took practice, but Melissa Penry has learned
how to get steady video without a tripod.

even notice the reminder any more; she does those things automatically when shooting a story.

Penry goes through several set-ups: she shoots from the back of the room, from the side of the room, from the front, over the shoulders of students, and even puts the camera on the floor for a low-angle view. She grabs wide shots to give the story perspective, medium shots to help in editing, and close-ups for telling details that will help bring life to the story.

Those details come out in the story she edited a few hours later. Penry juxtaposed close-ups of the student's jeans and sneakers against the spit-polished shoes and sharply pressed uniform trousers of the professional sergeant major teaching the JROTC class.

Discussing her conversion from reporter to VJ, Penry seems ambivalent. "I don't think my reporting has suffered," she laments. "I'm still a good reporter. It's just I have to multitask more."[2]

Chapter 5

Get Closer to Your Subject

Never forget that the best stories are about people, not just facts about an issue. You want to build stories around people your audience can relate to. That task begins by choosing good characters for the story and then working to get the best video and sound with them while shooting the story.

A solo videojournalist has a built-in disadvantage at this point in the process. Some things are just tougher to do alone than in a crew. Take interviewing, for example; in a two-person crew, the reporter can focus on the questions and getting the most out of the subject, while the photographer can make sure the shot is in focus, the subject is well lit and stays in the frame. Obviously, someone working alone in a video interview has to ask the questions and do the shooting as well.

Despite that drawback, there are some things that people working solo on a video interview might actually do better than a pair working to accomplish the same thing.

Put Your Subjects at Ease

VJs say that it is often easier to get people to open up more, get them to say things they might not have said, when it is just the two of them alone with a small camera. There is something about a threesome with a cumbersome tripod, big camera, and bright lights that sometimes diminishes an interview's intimacy.

"It's all about your relationship . . . the equipment shouldn't get in the way of that," says *washingtonpost.com* VJ Ben de la Cruz. "So, that's why these

Making interviewees comfortable on camera is one of the
VJ's primary tasks in getting good sound bites for a story.

small cameras have kind of fueled this solo videojournalism because it's less
imposing."[1]

Other VJs have had similar experiences. "There's no question that working
alone you get closer to people," says Pierre Kattar, formerly with *washington-
post.com*. With several years of experience as a videojournalist working both in
crews and by himself, he says it is usually better to approach people alone. "It's
all about relationships. It's all about trust. You have to build that."[2]

As a result, VJs may have a natural advantage in putting their subjects at ease.
In fact, when setting up a story and trying to find a compelling character, the
less intrusive one-on-one may be a selling point to persuade a source who is
reluctant to sit down for an interview. "Oh, it's just me and my little DV camera," you can tell the source. "There won't be a monster photographer with a
whale of a camera traipsing through your living room. I won't even need to set
up lights that will make you sweat."

The key is to gain the source's trust. The VJ needs to be sincere, however, and not just fake it. People will see through that. Plus, if you are saying things just to get an interview and video, but don't follow through on your word, you will lose the source's trust and respect.

To get that trust, as a journalist you need to take an interest in your source's problem or idea that makes them story-worthy. That does not mean you should become an advocate for their issue. Just promise them that while you are obligated to present a balanced story with multiple perspectives, you will be fair in telling their side. Then stick to that promise.

That's all most people want, just a chance to be heard. If you promise them a fair shot at presenting their story, that will go a long way to establishing a camaraderie with your characters and will help put them at ease for an interview.

Have a Conversation Instead of an Interview

Award-winning reporter Boyd Huppert of KARE-11 in Minneapolis says he rarely uses the word interview when asking someone to appear on camera. Even someone reluctant to be interviewed, he says, can be engaged in a conversation. "The greatest words in the English language for getting someone to cooperate with me," Huppert says, are "'would you help me with something?'"[3]

Whether on the phone setting up an interview or approaching someone in the field, just try to have a conversation instead of interviewing the person. Have some questions you want to ask, but don't force them on the person right away. Just listen to them; work the questions into the conversation in a natural way and they will start to open up. Once you do that, you usually will have all the information you need for the story.

Even though you will get a lot of information and background on the phone, save the best questions to ask on camera. Once you arrive at the location for the interview, it may help to set the camera aside for a short time and just keep chatting. Then, when it feels there is some rapport, it will be time to drag out the camera and other equipment and begin shooting.

Aim to get two (or more) interviews with the main character in a story. The first is a formal, sit-down interview, where you can get most of the information and often some good bites for a story. The second will come later as you gather video; just continue the conversation while posing some questions that you record along with other natural sound and video.

In formal sit-down or stand-up interviews, most people don't feel natural being hooked up to a microphone, having the barrel of a lens pointing at them, and squinting into a light, answering questions. If not the third degree, it must seem, at least, like the second degree.

Most people never will have been on camera in a professional interview. This is a chance to just continue the conversation you started earlier on the phone or when you first approached them at the scene. Rather than pump the person for the answers you need for the story, as you are setting up the camera, just chat about what you are doing to set up for the interview or something else going on in the person's life. Get the person used to talking to you even though you may not seem to be giving them your full attention as you are doing other things with the gear. KGO-TV San Francisco VJ Wayne Freedman says he tries to involve his interviewees in helping him set up the gear; just chatting with them while working helps him get to know his subjects better.[4]

Another way to ease the burden of the interview's technical requirements is to try to put the interview subject in a setting that helps put them at ease. That may be behind a desk where they would be working if you were not there. It might be in a lawn chair in the subject's back yard. Or, if their time is tight, you might accommodate them by just having them do a stand-up interview to get some quick bites.

Pay Attention to the Conversation and the Camera

Whatever the set-up for the interview, this is a crucial point in the process where the VJ has to pay equal attention to being both the reporter and the pho-

Sometimes sitting alongside the camera
can put subjects more at ease in an interview.

tographer. For the reporting, what should be asked and what are the responses? Listen to the subject's answers to see if they deserve a follow-up question. Is it the expected response? Is it truthful? Does it make sense? Does it disagree with what you or others know about the issue? Is it consistent with what this person has said in the past?

If the answer to any of those questions is NO, then the logical next question is "Why?" or "How?" Why do they disagree with the conventional wisdom? How can they say that when so many others are taking a different approach? Why are they backing away from their past position? How has their opinion on the subject evolved over time?

The answers to these questions may become key elements in writing the package later.

NBC correspondent Bob Dotson also uses an interview technique he calls the "Non-question/Question." Listen carefully to what people are saying then make a comment about the answer instead of posing a question. That might draw the interviewee into saying something very interesting and useful about your comment. Dotson also says instead of jumping right in with another question, a pause might elicit a longer and more revealing response from an interviewee.[5]

That Dotson technique may be especially useful if your goal is to do a natural sound package without narration. "Most of our stories feature good characters," writes *New York Times* video editorial director Ann Derry. "When a character is articulate, we try to let them tell his or her own story."[6] In those situations you want to get responses that are full sentences, complete thoughts. You will be able to edit those more easily into a story that requires no narration for context or background.

If you are having trouble getting the interviewee to talk in complete sentences or if they are getting too technical, don't be afraid to sound dumb. "If you ask someone to re-explain something, they will usually be a lot more descriptive," says Baltimore's Bryan Barr, who has produced a number of natural sound stories as a videojournalist.[7]

Another technique may be counterintuitive in an interview, but can be very successful: silence. Sometimes when an interviewee pauses he may be on the verge of saying something compelling. If you jump in at the pause with another question, it may ruin the moment. Silence at that point may encourage the interviewee to open up and say what is really on his mind.

A standard wrap-up question also may elicit a brand-new way to approach the story as well. After finishing all the questions you think are pertinent, ask: "Is there anything else you'd like to say?" Sometimes you haven't asked what the interviewee really wants to talk about; sometimes the answer to that innocent question will open a whole new line of inquiry that you had overlooked.

It doesn't happen often, but occasionally the answer may take your story in an entirely different direction.

The VJ Interview Technique

Since this is a crucial point in the multitasking environment, as the VJ listens and formulates questions, he never can take his mind off the camera. Is the shot properly framed, is it properly exposed, and is the sound just right? Lack of attention to any single element could ruin a moment—or the entire interview—that is essential for the story.

"You've got to be able to think about the camera and the shot and watch the person you're interviewing and whether they shift to the side and walk out of frame," says KUSA backpack journalist Dan Weaver. "At the same time you're listening to them answering your questions and you've got to be thinking of your next question at the same time. You've got to be thinking: do I have all the sound there that I need for this story? Doing everything at one time can be tough."[8]

When shooting a formal interview, first be careful that the background is not distracting, a plant growing out of the subject's head, or a window spilling too much backlight on the interviewee. If there are such distractions, find a better location for the interview.

Once they've found the right spot and the subject is in place, some VJs request that the interviews act like a rock, keeping every muscle still, or point to a spot on the floor and ask them to keep their feet planted so that it doesn't spoil the framing. That can help, but it might also make the subject an uneasy participant. Remember the goal is to get good information and sound bites; if the subject is told to freeze physically, they may freeze verbally as well.

So instead of making the subject part of the crew, make sure you are taking the responsibility to ensure you get pristine video and sound. Frame the person looking slightly off camera with their eyes about a third of the way from the top of the screen.

Wear headphones to make sure the audio stays clear—though you may want to leave one side cocked off your ear so you can hear the ambient sound of the room and make it appear that you are really listening to the subject and not just the camera.

Once the camera is rolling, take a half step away from the camera so the interviewee is not looking straight down the lens. Some Web VJs, however, prefer their interviewees to look straight at the lens, to let the audience have direct eye contact. This might be useful in situations where VJs are doing a personality profile without any narration to the piece.

In either method, try to keep your focus on the person as you are asking questions, yet stay close enough to the viewfinder to keep an eye on the framing and audio levels. If the subject moves, you will need to adjust the camera so that they stay in focus and in frame. The best time to do that is while you are asking another question, but if the subject moves too far from the proper frame while answering a question, be aware of that and pan or tilt the camera even while the subject is talking.

It also helps to have a camera that has a flip-able viewfinder, one that you can see from either in front of the camera or from the right side. That will give you optimum flexibility in shooting from either side of the camera so your interviewees face different directions.

Get the Two-Shot and Reverse

Once you've got all the answers you need in the formal interview, back the camera up for a two-shot. You may need it to set up the interview in the story. To help in covering a possible jump cut, also get a reverse shot over the shoulder of the interviewee, looking at you doing the interview.

When you do that, make sure you align the camera so that it does not cross the axis, the imaginary 180-degree line that splits the screen. Shoot the reverse shot so that the interviewee appears to be facing the same direction as during the interview. In other words, if the subject was facing screen left during the interview, move the camera to the right and shoot the subject just to the left of their back. Then go stand in front of the interviewee so that they are still looking in the same direction when the reverse shot is cut together with the interview.

Do an Informal Interview

Now that the formal interview is out of the way, get video of the person doing something to help illustrate their part of the story. One standard technique is to ask, "What would you be doing if I weren't here? Can I get some video of you doing that?"

Once they agree to continue their normal work, this is a good place to complete the interview while shooting your cover video. Here it will come out more like a conversation than the previous formal question-and-answer session. The character for your story will be in his element, doing something routine. The person should be getting accustomed to you and your camera by now. If you used a wireless microphone for the first interview, keep it on them now. While getting a few shots, slip in a comment or question about what they are doing; their response may make a good natural sound break. Rephrase a question from the formal interview; that may make a better, more conversational bite than one from the sit-down interview.

Get good natural sound of them working, yet use a few questions to amplify the subject's experience in a less formal way. While shooting a close-up, ask a question and zoom out or pan to the person's face; this will give you material to help edit the story in a natural flowing way.

Using a wireless microphone, such as this receiver mounted on top of
the camera, can make getting interviews and natural sound much easier.

Doing both the formal and the off-the-cuff video interviews will provide
different types of sound to work with and help you tell the character's story
when you sit down to write and edit the piece later. Of course, depending on
the circumstances of the story, you might also want to reverse the process doing
the off-the-cuff interview first and the formal interview after that. Just determine which way helps put your subject at ease and might be the more efficient
way to shoot the story.

One caveat, however, to getting the informal interview: don't keep chatting
while you are shooting the cover video. You also need plenty of natural sound
of the subject working that is not ruined by either of you talking over it.

Get Closer to Your Subject

Sure the zoom lens is a nifty little device that lets you get tighter perspectives
on subjects without ever having to move the tripod. That does not mean you
should rely on the zoom to get your close shots. Instead, adopt a commonly
used technique, "Zoom with your feet, not with your lens."

That means moving your camera and tripod up close to people or other subjects you are getting video of and using a wide angle instead of a telephoto shot
of the subject.

"I rarely ever zoom in and focus," says Kim Edwards in a video about digital correspondents at KGTV. "I actually walk into the person."[9] This has a couple of advantages. The wide angle will give a richer feel, a closer perspective as if you are sitting next to the subject instead of the narrow depth of field that a telephoto shot provides. When interviewing someone it also provides greater intimacy. You can talk to someone from ten feet away and zoom in to get just the right angle, but then you are doing an interview from a distance. Getting close, sitting next to the subject with the camera lens on wide angle, will make it easier to have a conversation instead of an interview—and perhaps get more intimate material from your story's character.

In a story about people getting tattoos, KGTV's Edwards says getting closer is the key to getting more intimate with the story's subjects: "I try to act like it, like this is a person at home watching TV and they're walking right up to the tattoo artist."[10]

Getting More Intimate Interviews

On some occasions former *washingtonpost.com* videojournalist Christina Pino-Marina found that working by herself resulted in a greater intimacy with her interviewees.[11] "It's as close as I'm going to get with working with a notebook and a pen," says the print-reporter-turned-VJ. "There aren't these distractions with a crew and a bunch of lighting and it doesn't feel like a big production."

She cites a time when she was doing a project on abused women. "It was such a delicate situation," Pino-Marina explains. She expected when she went to one shelter to get information on domestic violence that it would be difficult to get women to open up to her. She first interviewed the person who ran the shelter, then one of the victims. Then other women who listened in wanted to tell their stories as well. "And I feel like just having that camera and very minimal equipment . . . just me and the camera, and these people, it was so intimate. And they told me all kinds of details about their personal lives and the things they'd been through."

Woman after woman came forward to share their stories: "It was a really powerful experience actually. And for me too; I came away from that and felt 'Wow, I was touched by that.'" Pino-Marina concludes the results might have been very different, the intimacy might have been destroyed, if she had had to work with someone else in her crew.

Getting an Informal Interview with a Reluctant Subject

Getting up close to people while shooting cover video can be a great way to get your second, informal interview with the subject, or a way to surreptitiously interview someone who is reluctant to sit down in front of a camera for an interview.

The author shot a documentary, *A Bridge to Cuba,* over a six-year period, sailing to the island three times. Returning from Cuba the first time one of the boat's crew, Carolyne Sheets, began crying while being interviewed about a Cuban boy whom she met whose father left for the United States. It was a very touching and memorable moment in the story. Two years later, as the crew prepared to sail back to Cuba, Carolyne refused to do another sit-down interview about what she expected to accomplish on the trip and how she planned to help the then seven-year-old boy. She was afraid that she would embarrass herself by crying on camera again.

So, as Carolyne was stocking the boat's galley, the author, working as a solo videojournalist, shot video of her stuffing food into the boat's lockers. Since the quarters were so tight, the scene was shot from the shoulder, keeping the lens zoomed all the way out, putting the videographer and camera less than two feet away from the subject.

As Carolyne was engaged in her work, a natural conversation developed, chatting about the trip and what Carolyne hoped to do while visiting Cuba for the second time. Even though she refused a formal interview, in the close quarters, the informal interview got all the information and sound needed by just talking with Carolyne while she was distracted with her work. Since she was so used to the lone photographer walking around all the time, shooting video of whatever was happening and posing questions from time-to-time, the camera captured a revealing interview despite the subject's misgivings.

Swallow Your Trepidation about Getting Close

Some novice videographers seem squeamish about getting so close to their subjects. They are concerned about invading peoples' space or that the subjects will push them away. Indeed, there are times when a VJ will decide the subject is not ready to have the camera so close. But there are other times the VJ just has to put his or her emotions aside to do the best job possible and ease the camera into other peoples' space to document the event for the public.

At the BBC, solo VJ Tom Hepworth says that getting "close to the action" is a more intimate way of telling the story, yet "it depends really on the journalist who's doing the VJing. If you stand back, and are removed, you're not going to get in there. But if you get in close and develop that relationship with an interviewee, quite often you know, you have to spend time with people to warm up and open up."[12]

Glenn Hartong is a VJ at the *Cincinnati Enquirer;* his brother-in-law is a firefighter. Hartong has covered dozens of fires over the years, but once he covered a blaze that killed a firefighter in Colerain Township, where he was familiar with a number of the firemen in the company. As a professional he had to put his feelings aside to get shots of the anguished faces of the officers he knew and respected. "It's hard. I know these firefighters will feel I have intruded, but as a journalist I know I must document the emotion," he wrote later in an *Enquirer* article. "The sadness I capture allows our readers and our viewers to feel the emotion these firefighters feel."[13]

The technique of getting up close to subjects won't work with everyone in every situation. That zoom lens can be a handy tool. But normally solo video-journalists should establish camaraderie with their subjects and get them used to the idea that they are always linked like an umbilical cord to a camera and tripod—and then get up close and personal to get the best elements for the story as possible.

The key is to be sincere about your interest in people. Swallow your trepidation and get close to people with your camera. The results will be worth it.

Use a Notebook

Several VJs seem to eschew the idea of taking notes while shooting their story. Many use the camera as a notebook, rolling on information that may take valuable minutes to wade through on a deadline. Sure, the video can be a great back-up when the VJ's hands are not free to jot down a quote, name, or idea, but for a journalist, a notebook is an essential tool. Use it—not the camera—to record essential facts.

Another way to use a notebook is to outline the story as it progresses. "Definitely write your story in your head as you shoot, drive and interview people. Silently talk the potential lines of your story while you shoot, so you can just meld your pictures perfectly to your words," says former VJ, now NBC correspondent, Michelle Kosinski.[14]

Add to that: jot down your ideas before you forget them.

Even though your hands are tied up manipulating the camera controls, keep a notebook or piece of paper in a pocket or tucked into a waistband where you can get at it and write down information quickly and then return to shooting. If used well, the notebook can save time: looking up the spelling of a character's name instead of searching through the tape or memory card, jotting down an important fact, or writing a line of the story that comes to mind while composing a shot in the viewfinder.

Get those thoughts and ideas down on paper before forgetting them. A multitude of VJ tasks could rob your memory of valuable ideas and information. Keeping them on paper is a way to make sure you have them handy from the beginning of the process to the end.

Find Your Comfort Zone

There are two things VJs need to be comfortable with: the gear and themselves.

"You . . . really need to know the equipment you're using, the camera, so that you can quickly hop over behind the camera, reset up the interview, move the camera if you need to, refocus it and then get back out there to continue the interview," says Dan Weaver.[15]

"Practice setting up your camera gear—not just once or twice, but to the point where you can hold a conversation and seem completely at ease," writes KPNX-TV backpack journalist Lynn French. "As soon as you can't find where to plug in the microphone, your interview subject is going to think you don't know what you are doing."[16]

Using the tools of the trade—cameras, tripods, lights, microphones, phones, computers, notebooks—needs to become second nature to the VJ. Former Sacramento VJ Dan Adams suggests that if people want to break into the business: "Go out and be your family's videographer; shoot your vacations; do what you find interesting and put it on tape. And just do it and do it every day and start practicing and get an editing program, so that when you do get to a situation where you have to do something like this, you're already ahead of what everybody else is doing."[17]

Working on a deadline is no time to start thumbing through a camera manual or the help file of the nonlinear editor. Knowing your equipment thoroughly will help you get your work in on deadline and produce pieces with creative touches using techniques others might not have discovered.

"I learned that the more experience I had with the equipment, the better my material ended up at the end," says *Virginian-Pilot* VJ Brian Clark.[18]

Be Prepared for Your Working Environment

Having a methodical way to organize your equipment can also pay off in time savings. It might be a good camera bag with ample pockets where you can stash tapes, batteries, and cables. Or, videojournalist Becky Blanton suggests using a vest that holds everything you'll need within easy reach. And she adds, "Put things in the same pocket each time so you can find them without looking."[19]

Being comfortable with oneself is just as important as being organized and intimately familiar with your equipment. Practice helps you find your gear comfort zone, but borrow the tried-and-true Boy Scout motto, "Be Prepared," for everything else.

Going into an interview with someone who is knowledgeable about a topic when you haven't done any research on the subject can prove embarrassing. If you are unprepared in interviews with politicians, they often will control the situation, being able to say anything they want on camera. If you are prepared with research, you can ask pointed questions that will not allow politicians—or others well prepared by their PR machine—to merely use you to get their message out without being challenged.

Being prepared also means dressing the part for your story. If interviewing a businessperson: women, wear a professional-looking pantsuit; men, wear a shirt, tie, and perhaps a jacket. If you are interviewing a farmer, then blue jeans and a more casual shirt are appropriate. Always carry clothing that will protect you in the shooting environment: old shoes that you can wear in a flood, a sweater or overcoat you can throw on to protect yourself from inclement weather, a hat or sunscreen to ward off sunburn.

If you are not comfortable working in certain conditions you will rush your shooting just to find a place that is warmer, drier, or cooler. If you are not prepared to work under any conceivable shooting condition, your story may suffer because you rushed the shooting to be more comfortable.

Being prepared to handle any situation, whether an obstinate interviewee or inclement weather, is the mark of a true professional and will pay off in better storytelling.

Discussion and VJ Exercise

1. Why does physical closeness make a difference when interviewing a character for your story?
2. When is it appropriate to move in close to people to interview? What types of situations would not be appropriate to move in closer for interviews and cover video?
3. Find raw video of a news conference online. What kind of follow-up questions should have or could have been asked, but were not?
4. Get video of someone working at a task. Ask them questions as the camera is rolling. Practice getting the natural sound of the subject doing their work, then doing pans or tilts as you ask questions to focus on the subject for a natural, off-the-cuff interview.
5. In the community in which you work, what kind of extra clothing or tools should you carry to be prepared to shoot in any condition?
6. Why is a notebook important to a VJ? What kind of information can be captured on camera that does not require a notebook? What kind of information jotted down in a notebook can save the VJ time later in writing the story? When you are shooting, where is the best place for you to keep a notebook handy?

Chapter 5 Focus
Getting the Most out of Her Subjects

Her right foot angles out and kicks in like a dance step practiced over and over. But instead of a ballet, Heidi McGuire is closing the legs on her tripod, ready to move for yet another set-up.[1]

She hefts the camera and tripod and executes a *glissade* a few feet to where the new shot will take place. Heidi pushes her knee out to bump the Libec's leg open, *pirouetting* with the three-legged contraption as if it were a familiar dance partner.

Heidi has performed this dance hundreds of times as a solo videojournalist. In college she learned how to report, shoot, and produce TV news. When it came time to look for a job, however, she avoided openings looking for one-man bands at first, but "after sending out a hundred resume tapes," she laughs, "and getting one offer as a one-man band job, I was going to do it." So, after graduating from the University of South Carolina, she began her career at KSFY in

KUSA Backpack Journalist Heidi McGuire has worked as a VJ since her first job in TV news.

Sioux Falls, South Dakota, working alone in a bureau seventy-three miles from the closest interstate highway. After another job as a one-man band at Gannett-owned WFMY in Greensboro, North Carolina, her hometown, Heidi landed at a mecca for news videographers, KUSA, another Gannett-owned NBC affiliate in Denver. "After doing that job in South Dakota, doing that job in the bureau," she says, "I felt I could do that job anywhere."

At a Saturday morning meeting setting out the day's news topics, Heidi comes to work wearing a white shirt, black pants, and flip-flops. A blazer and slacks hang from the filing cabinet near her desk, and hiking boots are stashed nearby just in case she needs more substantial footwear.

As the meeting gets underway, beneath the 9 News logo over the curved assignment desk, Heidi is sitting, drinking coffee. The stories on the agenda include a ten-year-old boy who was killed in an overnight traffic accident, a local company's satellite rocketing into space, parolees cleaning up graffiti, and a rash of Ketamine thefts from veterinarians' offices.

Nicole Lewis, a producer, asks, "Do you want to do your accordion story?"

"Sure," Heidi replies. The BPJ estimates she has a story assigned only 10 percent of the time. She says one of the difficulties of working alone and having to do all her own reporting, shooting, editing, and filing stories for the station's Web site is finding time to come up with her own story ideas.

Even though she normally works alone, just like other reporters and photographers, Heidi is on call to cover breaking news once a week in the mornings and once a month on weekends. Then, however, she always works with another photographer. Once she was called out early in the morning to cover a tornado; she did twelve live shots and a package between five a.m. and noon. Though she covets her status as a backpack journalist, "There's always a place for two-person crews as well," she admits. "There are things two-people crews can do better, breaking news, spot news."

News vice president Patti Dennis agrees: "There's more hands to sort of help the workload. There's two sets of eyes: Did you get that? You need to go talk to that guy." So the solo videojournalists at KUSA usually do features or non-deadline stories where it's not as critical to have a crew of two.

And that's just the kind of story Heidi's been assigned on this Saturday, a festival for the Rocky Mountain Accordion Society. As she pulls up in her white Blazer marked with the station's blue and red logo, she moves to the back of the vehicle to prepare her gear. Along with the video camera and assorted other equipment, there is a virtual footlocker: five pairs of shoes, including one mesh and two pairs of waterproof shoes. The first thing she does is exchange her flip-flops for a pair of low-cut, black, ballet-like shoes, the perfect fit to perform a *pas de deux* with her camera/tripod.

She puts batteries in her wireless microphone receiver and transmitter, stuffs them into a fanny pack; she takes two sheets of white paper, folds them into fourths to use as a notebook and puts that in the fanny pack, too, then tucks headphones in the waist strap. She slings her Sony HDV camera over her right shoulder so the camera hangs at her hip. Over her head, she slips another strap for a Steady Bag onto her right shoulder so it dangles on her left hip, then onto the left shoulder goes the strap for the light kit. Finally, five-foot two-inch backpack journalist Heidi McGuire lifts her dancing partner, the Libec tripod, onto her right shoulder and totes it all toward the entrance of the hotel.

"Hi, how are you?" Heidi greets accordion player Paula Quintana, whom she had only talked with on the phone. Yet they hug as if they are long-lost friends. "I think Paula's going to be great," says Heidi. Going into the story, the focus is on this woman who started playing the accordion only four years before, but now is winning a slew of awards. Heidi wants to tap into that experience and tell the story through Paula's eyes.

The journalist says she likes to spend time getting to know people before she starts shooting video. "For that time that you are with people, it's almost like a relationship that you build with that person," she says. "Even if you have only so much time to do that, I think it makes such a big difference."

"Some people are a little bit more open to talking to me, either because I am by myself and feel bad for me, and I'll take it," she laughs. "Or because it's just me and I hope that I can make people feel comfortable and that my personality is oh, this is not just a reporter, this is a person."

Her boss, Patti Dennis, says there's something not only about Heidi's personality and size, but the style of working alone, that contributes to her success as a storyteller. "I think just based on her approach and her small packaging, everything from her smaller person to her smaller gear, people don't feel quite so threatened," says Dennis. "And so I think sometimes she gets interviews and access sometimes that other crews wouldn't get."

A gaggle of youngsters gather around as Heidi sets up to interview Paula in the hotel atrium. An odd mix of outdoor and indoor lighting makes for a tricky color balance, so Heidi gets an eager boy to hold a piece of paper for her camera's white balance, then gives the youngster a high 5.

She sets Paula in a chair, asks her to hold her accordion while doing the interview, then clips the wireless mic to the accordion strap. Four kids are standing very close to Paula within the camera shot. "I'm going to have you guys take a big step over this way," Heidi says, gesturing for them to move away from Paula. Then she drags a chair over near the camera, slides on headphones, and checks the audio levels in the viewfinder. "Are you comfy?" she asks, then sits in the chair, two feet to the front and left of the camera. After a few questions she gets up and adjusts the camera to make sure Paula is framed just right. During the interview, she rises one more time and hits the camera zoom as she asks another question, this time with Paula on a wide shot.

When the interview is over, Heidi readjusts the mic cord so it can't be seen and asks Paula to play something on the accordion. She puts on her headphones again and punches the start button on the Sony. "Whenever you're ready."

She gets a tight shot of Paula's hands scrolling over the keyboard, then a wide shot. "Keep playin'," she tells Paula, then moves the camera directly in front of her for more video. Very quickly she does seven camera set-ups: from the interview spot, over Paula's shoulder, lowers the tripod to shoot up at the accordion player, moves way back to get a telephoto shot with a flowerbox in the foreground, a wide shot from behind Paula, another over the shoulder, then right behind her.

That completed, Heidi removes the camera from the tripod, gets the Steady Bag and places it on the floor in front of Paula and takes several shots there: off the bag, then kneeling with the bag on one knee. Each time she finishes a shot, she looks away from the viewfinder and scans to look for another angle. She moves to the right and places the Steady Bag on a nearby table for another shot.

Heidi's ballet continues as she changes subjects. She asks Paula's seven-year-old granddaughter for an interview. She places Aurora, who is holding a briefcase-sized accordion, on a rock wall near a fountain. "I'll be right back, okay?" Heidi walks a few feet to retrieve the tripod. She slides the camera onto the tripod and carries both over. "You want to swing your leg around a little bit for me?" Then when she can't get the angle she wants, moves Aurora to another spot nearby. "That background's so blown out," she says.

When she gets the shot she wants, Heidi asks, "You want to play something for me first?" Heidi rolls continuously while Aurora plays, first getting a close-up of her hands, then moves the camera farther back to get a wide shot with the fountain in the foreground.

Setting up for an interview, she moves to the right of the camera. "How long have you been playing?" she asks, standing eighteen inches from the camera. "What are you doing? Tell me what you're doing," she says as Aurora responds by pulling the squeeze box out and back in again. Heidi poses one last question: "How do you spell accordion?" Aurora, wrinkles her brow, then responds, "a . . . c . . . I forget the rest."

After the interview, Heidi unhooks the mic, asks the girl for a high 5 and gets it.

Heidi's ballet for the accordion story is now in the second act. She arranges four chairs so three boys and a girl can play together. "Do you have a back pocket?" Heidi asks one boy as he stands to let her fit in the wireless mic transmitter. She asks them to play something, then lifts the camera and tripod and carries them off, taking the elevator up to the second level of the atrium to get some shots of the kids performing from above. She sets up in three different spots while they are playing.

When she returns to ground level, she kicks one tripod leg out with her foot, then lowers it to the kids' eye level for an interview. When finished interviewing one boy, she gives him a thumbs up and moves to another in the quartet. "How would you describe the sound it makes?" she asks. "A big sound," he responds.

One young girl watching the interview touches the leg of the tripod, but Heidi gently admonishes her "oops, don't touch" and gently nudges the girl's arm away. Without missing a beat, Heidi continues interviewing the young accordionist, "What are all these buttons and what are they for?"

For another on-camera interview, Heidi selects a woman wearing a crown. "Are you the accordion queen?" The queen plays a tune while Heidi rolls from seven different set-ups, front, side, back: all from the tripod. Finally, she puts the camera on the ground on top of the Steady Bag and aims up. Heidi finishes shooting the cover video, then conducts the interview from there, too, kneeling before the accordion queen.

In all of the interviews, Heidi smiles and listens intently. People find her very easy to talk to. When she is interviewing them, they seem to be the most important people in the world; she sometimes chuckles or laughs when the subject says something funny. She is totally engaged in the conversation and seems to let the camera gear take care of itself once she has it set up. "It's just TV news," says the backpack journalist. "You can't take yourself too seriously. If you have fun, people have a good time talking to you and you get good stuff."

Over the two-hour period Heidi has shot thirty-eight minutes of video, slightly over her target of thirty-five minutes of raw video for each story. "I didn't even know this existed," she says. "This has been fun. I've learned a lot today."

As Paula and Aurora pack up their instruments to leave, Heidi says, "It's been great. Thank you." Aurora says, "Bye, bye," then gives Heidi a hug. Heidi turns the camera toward the lobby where Paula and Aurora are exiting. As the pair climbs the short steps, Aurora turns to wave goodbye and Paula follows suit. This will be the closing shot to the accordion festival story.

As the deadline for her story looms, Heidi acknowledges one drawback of working alone. "I miss the efficiency. I'll be on stories with two-person crews and they'll be in and out of there before I am," she says. "Does that mean that because they get out of there sooner that their story is going to be better? Just because I stay longer, does that mean that my story is going to be better? Do we get the same job done? I don't know how you rate that. But I do feel that they're more efficient."

Chapter 6

Be One with Your Equipment

When shooting cover video for your story, all the rules that apply to a crew videographer still stand for the solo videojournalist as well.

If the video is shaky, out of focus, or dark, if the sound is over modulated, low or otherwise unintelligible, viewers aren't going to cut the VJ any slack: they don't know whether it was shot by a photographer working in a two-person crew or a VJ. They just know that the story is awful.

Follow the Rules to Get Useable Video

The production of the VJ story has to be just as clean as if it were shot by a person focusing only on the video and sound instead of multitasking as the reporter. Doing that requires both technical and creative skills. Remember, unless you do the A, B, C, and D of shooting correctly, you won't have the flexibility of writing and editing a creative a story later. Here are some specific rules to follow to ensure you have the requisite video for a well-told video story:

A. White Balance: Many of the newer cameras will do this automatically. Yet this step is essential to getting any useful video. If you trust the automatic white balance on your camera, that's great; otherwise, perform this manually. White balance when you first start shooting and re-balance every time there is a change in lighting conditions, such as opening the drapes in an artificially lit room. You might be able to color correct the video later using the nonlinear editing software, but if you don't get properly color balanced video in the field, you might also lose any chance of telling the story.

B. Get a Variety of Shots: This may seem obvious since, unlike a newspaper or magazine story, you need pictures to cover every word and every sound in the video. Sure a VJ could cover a 1:30 story with six shots that are each fifteen seconds long, but that would be boring. Novice reporters and videographers sometimes learn the hard way that they just did not get enough different shots to tell a complete story.

  Every shot should fill the screen with something interesting. Don't frame the subject too wide or too close, but find something that adds perspective to the story and lets the viewers see it in detail.

  Don't be lazy in the field. Do a number of different set-ups for each scene to get different views and angles to provide opportunities to edit a well-paced and compelling story.

C. Shoot Sequences, Not Individual Shots: While shooting a variety of shots your mantra should be "Wide shot, medium shot, close-up." Always shoot sequences to help edit the story later. You can reverse the mantra and start with the close-up, then shoot the wide shot or use any other combination in the sequence. But if you don't have the sequence of shots you won't be able to use it when editing the story.

  Besides shooting with your ears to listen for anything going on that may make better video, you also need to shoot with your eyes. If the action dictates it, you may need to get the tight shot before you get the wide shot so you don't miss a golden action opportunity.

  It is imperative to get cutaways, which are close-ups or reverse shots of a subject, or reaction shots of people or things that create a logically edited sequence. At each camera set-up shoot at least one cutaway you might need later to avoid a jump cut in the edited story. A jump cut is a shot that does not make visual sense when cut together with another shot. An example is a close-up of a person's face showing her wearing glasses; if the next shot is the same person without the glasses it would be a jump cut.

  The BBC trains its VJs to use the "five-shot rule." In following the action of someone working on something, the five shots would be (1) a close-up of the hands, (2) close-up of the person's face, (3) wide shot of the scene, (4) over the shoulder of the person performing the action, and (5) a shot from a different angle to show a new perspective.[1]

  The close-up of the person's face or the close-up of the hands in that five-shot sequence are cutaways from the main action in the sequence that could save you when you edit the story later.

  Hold each shot for at least ten seconds. If there is action, follow it from a logical beginning to its completion. If that is only five seconds, make sure you hold it longer at each end to give you ample flexibility in cutting the shot later.

  In some instances you may want to allow the action to go into or out of the frame. An example of this technique is while keeping the camera stationary, someone would walk across the screen, entering from the left and then exiting the picture on the right. It can be cut with other shots either before the subject comes into frame or after they go out of frame. That is a good way to avoid jump cuts and is especially useful in profiling people as they move from place to place.

If there is no action in the shot, you could get away with less than ten seconds, but might regret it later if you need one long shot to slow the pace and let the viewer absorb the story's information.

D. Look for the "Wow" Shot: Video can take the audience to places they can't go or would not want to go themselves. Once you get the required sequences to tell a complete story, look for different angles and perspectives to tell the story in ways viewers don't normally see things. That may be simply putting the camera on the floor for an extremely low angle; it may mean walking up six flights to get an overview wide shot of a fire from an adjacent building. Look for that one shot that will make viewers say to themselves, "Wow, look at that!"

Low angles can be the "wow shot" in a lot of stories. Former KXTV/News 10 Sacramento VJ Dan Adams did several stories about Highway 12, a road with a killer reputation. Adams was doing one more story about the state's effort to

Look for "wow" shots such as an extreme
low angle, as VJ Angela Grant is getting here.

make the road safer. He stood on the center line of Highway 12, placing his camera on the double yellow stripe to get a low-angle view—a wow shot for the story. "This is a shot people wouldn't be able to see," says Adams. "People don't lay down on the ground in the middle of a busy highway to see the line."[2]

There are other tried-and-true methods to turn an otherwise mundane shot into one more pleasing to the eye. Use the Rule of Thirds in framing. Think about a grid on the screen like a tic-tac-toe surface: frame the most interesting things on the screen at the intersection of those lines rather than placing them smack-dab in the middle of the shot. Another technique is using a strong foreground, an object nearer to the camera, to frame something of interest in the background. Along with the strong foreground, you can also use a rack focus—which changes the focus from one object to another while the camera is rolling—to draw attention to something nearer or farther in the shot.

E. Justify Your Camera Movements: Normally let the action happen on the screen instead of artificially producing it in the camera. In other words use camera movements, such as zooms and pans, sparingly. Our eyes don't have the ability to zoom in or out from an object that we are viewing and we normally fix on something that we are looking at instead of sweeping across it. So a story without zooms and pans will seem natural. Too many zooms and pans make the story look as if it were shot by someone who just received a video camera Christmas morning.

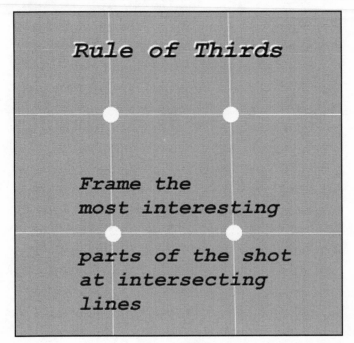

Rule of Thirds

Instead, let the action happen in front of the camera and then follow it.

If you do pans or zooms on static objects use them judiciously. If you decide either a pan or zoom is necessary, think first of how you will write copy for it and use it in the story. Then practice to get the smoothest possible result. If you do pan, start at a specific visual point and end the camera movement on another specific item after a short pan instead of sweeping the entire horizon. Don't use a herky-jerky zoom or a bumpy pan. If you do, it is a sure sign of an amateur.

F. Figure Out Your Opening and Closing before You Finish Shooting: The opening and closing are keys to a well-told package. If you don't have those in your mind and the video in your camera before leaving the scene, you will regret it when you sit down to write and edit.

The opening should help establish the scene. It should have great natural sound along with it to help grab viewers' attention.

It doesn't have to be a wide shot; it could just as well be a tight shot or medium shot that draws the audience in and won't let them go.

The closing shot gives viewers a sense that the story is finished. For example, it would make more sense to have someone walking away in a closing shot than walking toward the camera. It is especially effective to save something dramatic for the close that will resonate long after the story is finished.

G. Don't Overshoot: This may seem to contradict "Get a Variety of Shots," yet remember that the clock never stops. "I think all too often people overshoot things," says *Virginian-Pilot* VJ Brian Clark. "They'll come back and look at their footage and they'll be overwhelmed. Okay, I have all this stuff, what do I do with it?"[3]

One way to limit the amount of video you shoot is to use your notebook to record facts. Don't roll the camera on mundane background information that you can record just as easily on paper; use your camera to record sights and emotions that you cannot express as well in your own writing. That will save time recording and reviewing your video later, plus give you the best visual material to use in your story.

If you are on a tight deadline, wasting time shooting too many scenes you won't use, logging them when you get back to the office, and ingesting them into the computer are steps that will subtract valuable minutes from your other tasks. Find the focus for your story while you are in the field and you will find a balance between too much and too little video to write and edit the story.

Use the Tripod

Even a novice newspaper VJ knows steady camera work is required in storytelling. "The last thing you want is somebody to stop watching the video because they're getting a headache," says Jesse Vega of the *Fort Myers News-Press*.[4]

A tripod is essential for a videojournalist. Use it for every shot in which the subject is static. With modern lightweight cameras, a tripod adequate for the model of camera is also lightweight and easy to carry. Using it—or sometimes a monopod—is the sign of a professional.

There may be occasions, however, where the situation demands that you shoot without the tripod. It might be a fluid, breaking news situation where a tripod is impractical. Or it might be cases where the lack of space is an issue, or where you judge that the tripod might hinder you from getting better video and information in a one-on-one with a subject.

"It's always better to get the moment than to be on a tripod," says Darren Durlach, of WBFF-TV in Baltimore and a two-time winner of the National Press Photographers Association TV news photographer of the year award. His motto is to shoot the moment first, get the sound that will make a difference in the story, then if necessary, shoot something later from the tripod that will help clean up the video for the story.[5]

In situations where you can't or don't want to use a tripod, you have to make sure that the shooting is as rock solid as possible. "I believe that comes with practice," writes Oregon VJ and blogger Cliff Etzel. "Shooters—if they are serious about the quality of their content—should learn to find that balance—it should look like it's hand held, but not be so obvious the viewer gets motion sickness."[6]

Until you learn to keep the camera steady, make sure you use a tripod as Jesse Vega of the *Fort Myers News Press* does.

Once you get the knack of shooting from the tripod, practice shooting from the shoulder or balancing the camera on other steady surfaces. The key is to keep the video steady. Even though sans tripod occasions may be rare, practice keeping the camera steady in different situations so you will be ready to shoot off the shoulder when you have to.

Ways to help reduce camera shake include the following:

Keep the lens on wide angle to minimize image movement.

Place the camera on the floor, a table, or other solid surface.

Carry and use a Steady Bag or your equipment pack to stabilize the camera.

Lean against a wall or other vertical surface to stabilize your body.

Keep your feet spread apart and your arms tucked into your chest to steady your body.

Hold your breath when rolling video. Every breath you take expands and contracts
    your body, shaking the steady platform you had hoped to create.

Be Aware of Lighting Limitations

Today's DV cameras often work well with natural lighting alone. But the video comes out better when the shooter is aware of the camera's limitations and deals with them. For example, having the sun behind a subject, called backlighting, can cause it to be silhouetted, unusable in normal video storytelling. An exception to the rule is if the VJ plans to purposely silhouette a person to disguise the identity of a subject who wants to remain anonymous.

Shooting at the source of the light can also cause lens flares, which are colored circles that appear in the image. So, avoid shooting into windows from inside; lower the blinds, move the subject, or move the camera so that you can eliminate the backlight, which will throw your subject into shadow.

If you can shoot with the existing lights, often the video image will appear more realistic and subjects won't be interrupted with the time it takes to set up a three-point lighting kit or be blinded by a camera-mounted light. But overhead lights can also give interviewees dark circles under their eyes from shadows cast by their brow. So be aware of this raccoon look and correct it if necessary with another lighting source.

Properly Expose the Image

One way to get the proper exposure is to zoom into the most important part of the scene you are shooting while the camera is on automatic exposure. Then flick the switch to manual exposure and zoom out again to frame the interview or scene as you like. Check the entire frame in the viewfinder, however, to make sure there are no parts that are too light or too dark.

Using a camera's zebra stripes can ensure that the scene is properly exposed. Without getting too technical, when engaged on a professional video camera, where the stripes appear in the viewfinder indicates that those parts of the image are overexposed. Not all cameras have the function. Check your camera's operating manual to see if they are available and for details on how to use zebra stripes properly.

Although it is better to make sure the scene is well lit while shooting, the editing software might also help improve the video. "There's hardly any shooting sin that you can't fix in editing," says award-winning VJ Mara Schiavocampo. "I try to remember that so I'm not too hard on myself if something is not exposed properly or the color's not right."[7]

One ethical caveat, however: use the editing software to change only the technical content of the video, not anything that will change the editorial substance.

Extra Lights May Be Necessary

There are times when setting up extra lighting will be crucial to making sure the video is usable for the story. Get a lighting kit and familiarize yourself with the typical three-point light set-up: the key light, fill light, and back light. Get used to using barndoors, gels, and umbrellas for lighting effects that are easier on the eye. Use the umbrella in a light kit to diffuse the harsh light for a pleasing natural effect. If you don't have an umbrella, you could also bounce the light from a ceiling for a diffuse lighting effect.

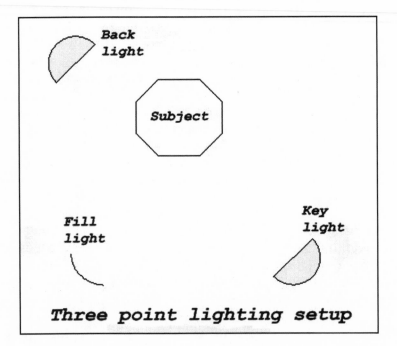

VJs should become familiar with a three-point lighting set-up for interviews.

You could also utilize a single light for a dramatic side lighting effect if the story calls for it. If you have a fourth light in your kit you can also use that with gels to make a more pleasing background as well.

In some cases you may be interviewing a dark-skinned person who has light-colored clothing. This is a prescription for major contrast issues that the camera won't be able to handle. Knowledge of different lighting techniques could help. Use barndoors on the key light to highlight the subject's face and keep light from spilling onto his clothing. Use a half scrim—a mesh filter that fits over the light to cut its intensity—on the lower part of the key light to illuminate the face more than the clothing.

Using a camera-mounted light—often called a "sun gun"—is the last resort since it results in a very flat, sometimes washed-out image that makes the background unrecognizable. But sometimes using the camera light is the only way to get a useable, well-lit image. If possible, bouncing the light off a ceiling will help reduce harsh shadows on the subject and appear more natural. You might try mounting the light a bit to the side of the camera as well, so that it doesn't produce such a harsh shadow directly behind the subject. Many of the camera-mounted lights also have dimmers that can reduce the harshness of the lighting. Use the dimmer so that the image on screen will appear as natural as possible.

Other Camera Controls for Lighting

Once the exposure is set, often it is best to shift from automatic iris to manual iris. This is useful outdoors shooting on a partly cloudy day; putting the iris on manual will keep the lens diaphram from opening and closing if there is a shift in light intensity while rolling. That will keep the video from going from lighter to darker and back again.

Some photographers also close the iris a half stop from the automatic exposure to provide better color saturation in the video.

There are a wide variety of techniques to shooting a quality video story. Take one and practice it until it becomes second nature. Then move on to another skill and then another; practice each one until you master it. Soon you will have a repertoire of videography skills you can use when you need them for your stories.

Discussion and VJ Exercise

1. Make a list of the things that you can control manually with your camera (such as shutter speed and audio levels). Do you know how to adjust them properly for various shooting conditions? If not, read your camera manual and practice using those manual controls. In what situations would you want to use the manual controls rather than let the

camera set the functions automatically? In what situations would it be better to let the camera automatically control the functions?

2. Practice hand-holding your camera while shooting video. Find the best way to shoot steady video by trying the techniques listed in this chapter. Which is the steadiest? Which technique is best for various shooting situations? Is there any technique that provides video as steady as that shot from a tripod?

3. Get a light kit and practice setting up a three-point lighting scheme. Also practice using a bounce light from a single stand as well as an umbrella reflector. Try using a "sun gun" mounted on the camera. Which provides the best lighting for various situations?

4. Set up a camera to do an interview with a person standing with their back to a window. What happens when the camera is left fully on automatic? How can you correct this situation?

5. Practice shooting a variety of shots. Find an object and do at least six camera set-ups. At each set up get at least a wide shot, a medium shot, and a close-up. During one of the set-ups make sure you get a "wow" shot

Chapter 6 Focus
The VJ's Equipment Bag

There is no such thing as a single list of equipment that a VJ can use. As shown throughout this book, what cameras, tripods, or nonlinear editors a VJ uses depends on his or her equipment preference or their organization's budget.

Yet there are two things that all VJ equipment should have in common: (1) it should be lightweight, and (2) it should be dependable. The quality of the video resolution on the camera will depend on what medium the VJ is shooting for, but frankly, any camera that shoots video can work in a pinch—even a cell phone camera.

Beyond that, it boils down to preferences and money. Do you like Final Cut Pro but find Avid editing systems more to your taste? Do you like the Panasonic P2 cameras, but find the Sony codecs work better with your editing system? Did you start shooting with a still camera and now want to continue shooting high-definition video on a DSLR (Digital Single-Lens Reflex) camera? No matter your preferences or budget, just like death and taxes, there is one sure thing about equipment for solo videojournalists, as soon as you buy a piece of gear, something will come along very soon that will outdate it.

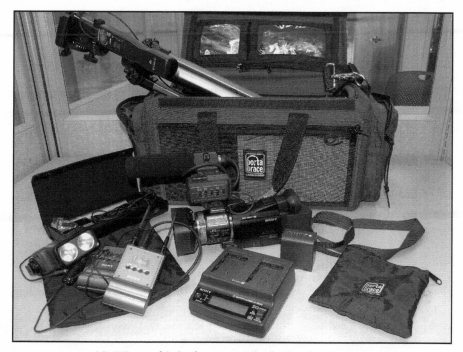

No VJ gear kit is the same. The basics, however, a
camera, tripod, and microphone will get the job done.

Nevertheless, the basic requirements for a VJ are these: a camera; a shotgun
microphone for natural sound from the camera; a wireless mic for interviews
and gathering natural sound from a distance; tripod; batteries; tapes or digital
media to record on; earphones to monitor audio; and, if needed, lights to shoot
indoors. If you choose to shoot with a DSLR, it needs a place to plug in a microphone rather than using the mic mounted on the camera body. A nice bag
and cart to carry it all around in come in handy as well. Editing also requires a
computer—either a desktop or laptop—and nonlinear software.

The equipment costs will set the VJ back about $6,000 to $10,000.

Cliff Etzel, who blogs about solo videojournalism and manages the Web site
solovj.com lists his preferences for equipment:[1]

- A couple of SONY HC7 HDV camcorders that shoot tape outfitted
  with SONY A1U lenshoods
- Azden SMX10 Stereo condenser mic
- Samson Airline Micro wireless lavaliere mic
- Audio-Technica wired lavaliere mic
- Bogen 3001 tripod with fluid head
- Century Optics wide-angle lens

Etzel writes: "The kit I've assembled for myself is a solid setup and can do a lot of what the bigger boys can—but in a smaller package." This is what's in NBC VJ Mara Schiavocampo's equipment bag:[2]

- A Sony HVR-V1U HDV camcorder, which is standard issue at NBC
- A Rode AA-battery-powered shotgun microphone
- Sony wide-angle conversion lens
- A lightweight Libec tripod, as well as a monopod
- A Litepanels MiniPlus camera-mountable LED light balanced for daylight
- XLR cables and XLR adapters
- Two wireless lavaliere microphone sets

At KUSA in Denver, backpack journalists use Sony HVR-Z1Us, says the station's photography chief, Eric Kehe. For stories that have a higher visual requirement, KUSA videojournalists use the Sony DSR-450/500 cameras.[3]

Since sound is so important in stories, never forget about the importance of quality microphones and headphones or earpieces to monitor the audio quality. "I could never, ever live without my wireless microphone and my earpiece," says Michelle Michael of the Armed Forces Network Europe. "I monitor audio at all times."[4]

As for editing, Etzel likes a Dell running Vegas Pro 8.[5] Schiavocampo carries a MacBook Pro with Final Cut Pro to edit.[6] But there are many other editing solutions on the market, too. Windows computers usually come stocked with Movie Maker and Macs have the iMovie software. Those are cheap—if not full featured—ways to edit video stories. Other, more full-featured, software packages for editing include Adobe Premiere, Pinnacle, and various Avid nonlinear products.

Chapter 7

Always Write to Get to the Next Piece of Sound

There's an adage that has circulated for years in TV newsrooms: the story is what you have on tape (or on whatever medium you recorded your video). If you don't have a bite of the mayor, you can't use it in the story. If you didn't get a shot of the landfill that is being closed, you can't write it in the package. If you don't have pictures of it, you may have to create a graphic to use the information in the package, or save the information for the anchor tag of the story.

"It's not the pictures and it's not the words. It's the story," writes WWNY-TV news director Scott Atkinson. As a small-market news manager in upstate New York, Atkinson has hired many people straight out of college as solo videojournalists who still need seasoning on their first job. He says he stresses storytelling to his rookie VJs "because it helps young reporters think about the pictures, sound and words as one thing, rather than two things to be picked between."[1]

This chapter focuses on writing a good video story: making a clear, well-told story by narrating it with the reporter's voice. As noted above, the person sitting down to tell this kind of story has to start by "writing to the pictures."

Since you are a VJ who has followed the "sound advice" tips for reporting and shooting in the field from previous chapters, there should be no excuses. If you shot with your ears, got plenty of sequences, and checked out the equipment before shooting the assignment, there should be plenty of video pieces to work with to assemble your story puzzle.

Video	Audio	CG1	CG2	VT	Time	Runtime	Date
PKG	PKG				1:37		3/23/2010 9:27

≈((NAT/SND coughing TRT=02)) @20:33

WE USE OUR HANDS TO COVER OUR COUGHS AND WIPE OUR NOSE...AND WE ALL KNOW GERMS EXPECTED.

@5:56 <Professor Rob Knight: "Overall, we found the equivalent of about 5,000 bacterial species and of thos

THE STUDY ALSO FOUND THAT WOMEN HAVE MORE BACTERIA ON THEIR HANDS THEN MEN...AND

@8:39<Valerie Donigian: "The only way I could believe it, is if I put it in the terms that women do more stuff,

@16:07≈((NAT/SND water running TRT=01))

SHE WASHES HER HANDS ALMOST A HUNDRED TIMES A DAY...BUT DR. MARIA ROSSI DOESN'T THIN

@12:13<Dr. Maria Rossi: "I think it probably has to do more with nail length">

BUT DON'T THINK THAT THIS THEORY CANCELS OUT THE DAILY ROUTINE OF KEEPING YOUR HANDS

@15:46≈((NAT/SND scrubbing hands TRT=01))

Whether using commercial scripting software or a word processor, writing a story is like editing it in your mind. Time codes in the script help in editing the story later.

Log Your Video

Now comes one of the most tedious—but also one of the most important—steps in the process: logging your video. As a VJ you should have a good sense already of what is on your tape or card. Yet you may not have recognized all the nuances of what you shot. Logging the tape is the only way to know whether that great bite you think you have is eight seconds or twenty seconds, if the natural sound can work in a sequence or whether the words you have in mind will work with the closing shot for the piece.

Logging is not a luxury. Unless you are on an extremely tight deadline, logging is an essential tool to let you examine in detail the pieces of your puzzle.

If you shot with your ears, there should be plenty of good sound to work with.

Use the time code to log the in and out points of both interview bites and natural sound. As you listen to the interviews, think of how short snippets of longer bites can be used to set up a sequence with the subject. That short bite might also come in handy to begin or end a sequence or be part of a dramatic close. Think of using your natural sound just as you do your sound bites from interviews. Does the faucet drip every two seconds or every six seconds? If it is the latter, you might be able to park a four-second piece of narration or a sound bite between the natural sound drips. As you shot video of your subject working and asked her a question, what was the length of time between her comment and when she continued typing on the keyboard? Should that be one continuous piece of video and sound, or should you break it into two pieces?

Each segment of sound, every worthy shot, the standup, and voiceovers are story components, pieces of the puzzle, that will help construct the overall picture and mood as you want it to look and feel. Just as shooting the story required technical and creative skills, now with the pieces of the puzzle logged, you have great flexibility to create a story with infinite variety that is only limited by your imagination.

Logging has one more advantage, too. Since you know exactly what pieces you want and which ones you can disregard, it will save time in capturing the video when you start to edit the story later.

Every Story Has a Beginning, Middle, and End

Once all the logging has been accomplished, there is no universal way to write a well-told story. Yet writing the story is editing the video in your mind, visualizing how the story will ultimately look once finished.

Logging, as Heidi McGuire is doing, is a crucial step
in getting to know the pieces of your story puzzle.

For traditional TV packages, the beginning point of writing may be different for each story. One might have a great ending narration and sequence in mind and build every piece of the story to get to that point. Some respected TV reporters begin writing in the middle and build from there.

Yet for the viewers, every story has to start at the beginning. That's why it is often best for the VJ to begin building the story there. If you lose your viewers at the beginning, they won't be around to watch that great sequence you constructed to end the story. So you've got to grab the audience and not let them go right from the start.

The Gateway to the Story

For a TV story, the anchor introduction is the gateway to the rest of the story. It could be a hard lead for a breaking news story, a soft lead for feature stories. If doing a narrated package for the Web, there still needs to be something that will grab the viewers' attention on the page. That could be a great still photo or graphic, plus a line or two of on-screen text setting up the video.

For either type of story, the gateway should have a great hook, with some intriguing informational bait that won't let the audience go. Or think of another metaphor: the anchor lead or Web site introduction is the aroma from the kitchen that whets the appetite; the VJ package is the four-course meal that satisfies the video-hungry diner.

Whichever way you want to think of the lead, there are ways to make sure it is as effective as possible. First, keep the language conversational. Write it as if you were talking to a buddy over a beer. Even before you write the lead, trick yourself into being conversational. TV news writer Abe Rosenberg calls this the "Invisible Lead." He writes that you should say to yourself, "Hey, you'll never guess what I just heard." Then, start writing the lead from there.[2] That approach will keep you from writing a dull, institutional type of set-up to the story.

Don't Get Complicated

Once you are in that frame of mind, keep the facts in the lead to a minimum: just enough to make the audience care about what is going to happen next and make them stay tuned, but not enough to give the story away and make them tune out.

That is the essence of another TV newsroom adage, "So What?" If the audience shrugs its collective shoulders and tunes out because you haven't written the lead to pique their curiosity, all your hard work is for naught. Intrigue your audience from the very first line. Famous names are okay in the lead, but don't use unfamiliar names as if the audience should know who they are. In other

words, saying, "Authorities have arrested John Doe for securities fraud," will just receive a "so what?" response. On the other hand, if you say, "Martha Stewart is going to prison for a securities conviction," the audience is more likely to sit up and pay attention.

If you don't show the audience right away how the story will affect them, they may tune out, asking, "Who cares?" Yet it is also smart not to give too much away in the lead about what part of your audience is affected. If you lead with "Property taxes are going up in Indianapolis," viewers in the market's other cities, Anderson, Carmel, or Greenwood, will respond by saying, "Who cares?" and tune out. A generalized lead such as "Property taxes are heading higher in one area community," will likely keep the audience tuned in long enough to see if it will be their pocketbook that is taking the hit. A good VJ would also check in that instance to see how other communities are affected and include that in the story, perhaps the anchor tag or on the station's Web site.

Once the first sentence establishes why the audience should care and pay attention, the second sentence should establish where the package is going and who the reporter is: the gateway to a remarkable story with impact.

The key at this stage is, do not overcomplicate the lead. Keep it simple. All you need are a few details, the appetite-whetting aroma that will keep them in front of the screen salivating for more.

Find Your Story Focus

"If you force them to listen, watch and learn, you're going to have more of an impact," says Emmy-winning TV reporter Elizabeth Hashagen.[3]

Previous chapters covered how to gather video and sound that will have impact—arousing a feeling, whether happy or sad—in viewers. Now it's time to organize the story to make sure it does have that effect.

Many journalists just turn in reports. That's okay. That is their job. They are paid to be reporters; sometimes the events they cover don't really lend themselves to meaningful storytelling on a tight deadline. Yet the best reporters—VJs included—will find ways to turn a mundane *report* into a real *story* that will have impact.

Chapter 3 talked about finding real-life characters to be part of the story. Assuming you've already done the critical work of finding strong characters who have experienced something newsworthy and shooting the necessary interviews and video to illustrate their relationship to the issue, how do you weave them into the narrative to achieve the most memorable tale?

Every good story should have a beginning, middle, and end. The writer should weave the theme, or focus, of the story throughout each segment. KARE-11 reporter, Boyd Huppert, says finding the focus is critical in TV storytelling: "Once I know it, it's so much easier to write the story. It tells me how to start the story; it tells me how to end the story."[4]

Come "Full Circle" in a Story

Having a main character is a way to help focus the story. Ideally the main character should be woven throughout, but especially at the beginning and end of the package. This is the "full circle" approach, sometimes called bookends. Along the way you should use sound bites from characters that evoke emotion or interpret conflict.

Use the story's characters to illustrate larger issues. Those people may be a microcosm of an issue or problem that could affect hundreds or millions more

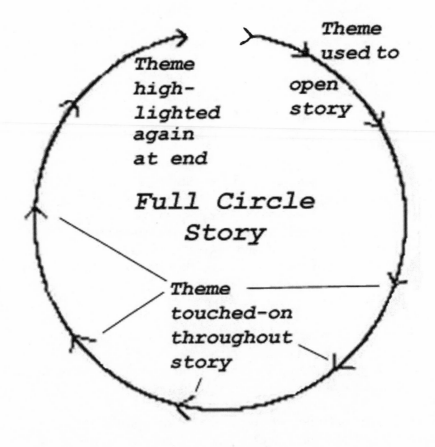

Full Circle story

people. The main character is likely involved in a conflict or controversy and is at odds with another person or group. The conflict between the two sides (or even more sides) keeps the audience in suspense and maintains their interest in the story.

In this full circle model, the story's beginning highlights the main character, why he or she is a sympathetic person with a problem we should care about. As the story progresses, we see why the character's position is at odds with others. Toward the middle of the tale we find out that this is not so rare; that indeed, many more may be facing the same dilemma as our main character. Here is where the VJ would insert background details and bites from experts. Or the story could show others who are involved, yet are not central characters in the story. Toward the end, there is either resolution to the issue or discovery that the dilemma is ongoing. This is the place to bring the main character—or protagonist—back into the picture, to see how she or he is dealing with victory or defeat.

Formulaic? Yes.

Effective? Probably.

Open to variation? Always.

Sound Is the Skeleton of the Story

Keep in mind that the goal is to have maximum impact on the audience. To achieve that, rather than write, and write, and write, and write and write and write . . . instead, *always write to get to the next piece of sound as soon as possible.* Limit your narration; let the sound bites and video with natural sound breaks carry most of the burden.

When you do write, make sure you have the video or a graphic to cover it. Visualize how one sentence will flow into the next with the pictures you have logged. Imagine how a natural sound break will lead easily into a sound bite. Visualize how another piece of natural sound can be a transition to the next part of the story. See in your mind's eye how your words, sound, and pictures will rise to a climactic ending with impact that will leave the audience in tears or glee.

The sound is the skeleton for the story. Choose your bites and natural sound first and build the story around those. Then, write to get to the next piece of sound as soon as possible.

The following imaginary full-circle story has Joe Doe as the main character, a government spokesperson who can put the negative information into context, plus a few man-on-the-street (MOS) characters to add more sound bites and prove that the main character is a microcosm of a wider trend:

Anchor Intro

Anchor on camera	Many people these days are struggling to make ends meet.
	Federal officials say the national debt is at its highest level since World War Two. As a result, Veejay Storyteller shows us that some Americans are digging deeper into their pocketbooks to help the country get out of debt.

Video   Narration and Sound

Video	Narration and Sound
Close-up of Joe's hand pouring a cup of coffee	Nat/snd full: coffee pouring for :02
WS of Joe with cutaway of hand putting coffee pot back	VJ narration: Every morning Joe Doe wakes up at three a.m. to get ready for his first job of the day.
Sound bite over video of Joe sipping his coffee	Joe: "I work three jobs just to keep my family fed and pay for my triplets' college tuition." :03
Close-up: hand on ignition key	Nat/snd full: car starting :02
Sequence in the car of Joe driving to work	VJ narration: Doe is out the door and on his way to his first job no later than 3:30. It's the start of what will be a 17-hour workday—the kind of hours he puts in six days a week.
Sound bite	Joe: "I don't mind working so hard, but I sure hate paying all those taxes. And what's worse, since I'm earning more than $100,000 in my three jobs, the government put me in a higher tax bracket so they are taking twice as much as before." :11

Continue sequence in the car then sequence of IRS building	VJ narration: Doe is not alone in this dilemma. The Internal Revenue Service estimates there are at least 13 million others working more than one job to make ends meet.
Sound bite (MOS)	Jerome Everyman: "It's rough, man. It seems like I'm at work 30 hours a day." :05
Sound bite (MOS)	Cicily Workman: "Everyone's gotta do more just to get by these days. I wish I could get another job." :06
Sequence of people getting off a bus stop	VJ narration: Many people are working extra jobs just to pay new taxes that Congress has imposed. Federal officials say they need the extra money to shore up the ailing Social Security system and pay down the national debt.
Sound bite	Social Security spokesman: "Without readjusting the Social Security payments, the system will run out of money in three years. There will be no money left for anyone's disability or retirement." :08
WS Joe at cash register	Nat/snd full: ka-ching of the cash register :01
Sequence of Joe at the cash register, ending with close-up of him putting money into the register	VJ narration: After four hours at this convenience store, Doe will head to his second and third jobs of the day. He knows he's just one of millions trying to pay the new taxes—but he has found a solution:
Medium shot of Joe coming out of the convenience store door and the door slamming behind him	Nat/snd full: door slams closed :02
Continue shot following Joe to his car	VJ narration: Doe has signed up for one more job, his fourth—this one just to pay the taxes on all the others. Veejay Storyteller reporting.

This story is oversimplified, but it makes the point about writing to get to the next piece of sound as soon as possible. No more than two sentences go by without the next piece of sound coming up.

"Every section, every possible place I can put extra sound, I do," says NPPA award-winning VJ Dan Weaver. "And that's both interviews, short bits of natural sound of people talking, yelling, or screaming as well as just the ambient natural sound, whether it's thunder or it's wind or somebody rifling through a rack of clothes. I think it's that constant sound that helps bring viewers into the story. And I guess it helps the stories just become real, come alive."[5]

What Makes Good Sound?

If you haven't got the point by now, even in video storytelling, sound bites and natural sound—not video—are the primary pieces to construct the story puzzle. But there are good ways to use the sound and there are not-so-good ways to use it.

In a typical 1:30 package there are two key elements that make interview sound bites stand out. The absolute best bites are short and emotional.

There are times when you want a two- to three-second bite just to set up a segment and introduce a person in the story. But if the bite is shorter than six seconds, that may not allow enough time to have a super to identify the person speaking. In an interview, people may take an extremely long time to explain their position or go off on tangents that have nothing to do with the main point of the sound bite. You will need to cut those down to a more manageable length.

When using an interview, let the subject express just one thought per sound bite. If it starts running longer than ten seconds, then viewers' minds begin wandering to something else besides the story. If you get to sixteen seconds, the audience may start heading for the refrigerator. A good bite can make a valid point in a short amount of time. So, the *optimum* time for a good sound bite is six to ten seconds.

Of course, there are always exceptions. If you have a much longer bite that is so compelling that cutting it would hamper the story, then use the longer bite.

The Hierarchy of Sound Bites

Everyone has seen an emotional sound bite on video that just could not be expressed nearly as well in writing. This is video's strength, experiencing the depth of someone's emotion through sight and sound. In the hierarchy of sound bites, choosing something emotional is at the top of the list.

Obviously, not every sound bite in a story can be, or should be, of that type. So, the second tier in choosing a sound bite is a multiple category of witness/perspective/opinion. If someone witnessed something and is adept at describing it in vivid detail on camera, the retelling of that experience would make an excellent bite. If a person has a unique perspective of a concept or view of life, their ability to express that might make a good bite as well. And, especially in stories in which conflict and controversy take center stage, a boldly spoken, heart-felt opinion or reaction can make for a compelling segment in the package.

The last type of bite to choose would be one that lends authority to the story. It might be an official who admits malfeasance; it could be a police officer explaining why crime is up or down; it certainly could be an expert explaining a complex issue in simple, understandable terms. Even if the VJ attributes such information to authoritative sources in the narration, it may not have as much credence as well-phrased bites from those types of people.

If there are facts that are essential to the story, sound bites are usually the worst way to get them across. A laundry list of facts is not the best use of a bite. The writer and skilled announcer can usually present them in a way that will hold the audience's attention in a more succinct manner than a sound bite. Instead of video, perhaps a multipart graphic is a better way to cement those facts in viewers' minds as well.

Writing into and out of Your Sound Bites

Let the pieces of interview you choose as bites illuminate the key points and issues of the story. They should continue the narrative flow of the story and improve the pacing. The narration setting up the bite should amplify and enhance it; the script should not repeat information that will be in the interview. One way to do that is to look at the log sheet, select information that the interviewee said before or after the sound bite and use it to set up the bite. That can give the bite the context it needs without parroting it.

This is where a meticulous log sheet can really help.

Sometimes it is useful to place bites with juxtaposing ideas back-to-back. This is a good place to show how a story's protagonist and antagonist are related, yet are at odds with each other.

After the bite or bites, the natural sound and narration should flow logically, continuing the storyline; it may be helpful to borrow a word or phrase from the previous bite to help the story flow seamlessly back into the narration. Write the segment to set up the next piece of sound that propels the story's theme to the next logical point. But don't use bites just to fill time. If you can write something better, with more clarity than a bite, then do it.

A word of caution, however, in choosing your bites: be critical of the sound quality. If you have trouble understanding what is being said, your audience will, too. You have the luxury of listening to the bite over and over; the audience does not. If you can't understand it because of muffled sound, a heavy accent, or a noise in the background, don't use it. If a bite with a heavy accent is critical to the story, perhaps you should use a translator or use text over the bite so that the audience will comprehend what is being said.

Punctuate with Natural Sound

Your VJ pieces should always use natural sound under the voiceover narration. But now that you have logged your natural sound just as diligently as your interview bites, you can use natural sound breaks—sometimes called "nat pops"—as punctuation marks, a method to improve the pacing and as transitional material from one point in your story to another.

"If you don't have good natural sound pauses, you're going to sound like a run-on sentence," says Michael DelGiudice, an award-winning videographer at WNBC-TV known for his video essays.[6]

Use your best pieces of natural sound to keep the audience engaged and to illustrate concepts. "Natural sound sets the pace; it also provides the proof," says KARE's Huppert. "I cannot say it, I cannot write it, unless I can prove it. And I prove it with natural sound."[7]

Natural sound breaks in the story can accomplish three things: (1) transmit the experience for the audience, (2) redirect their focus back into the story as attention spans wane, and (3) serve as a transitional device from one part of the story to another.

Video can be lifeless without the sound. Even foreign movies don't need translation or subtitles when it comes to images with sound that transcend spoken language. The aural element creates a sense for the audience that they are sharing what they see on the screen with those who actually lived it. Use natural sound and video collected on the scene of the event to transmit what it was like to really be there.

Nat pops are also useful in preventing the audience from drifting away. Predictability is a storytelling sin. Why watch or listen if we already suspect what is going to happen? Media savvy audiences surely know the typical structure of a TV package: narration, sound bite, narration, sound bite, narration, sound bite, standup. Predictability makes the audience complacent. Unexpected natural sound breaks with lively video are like bombs tossed at the audience's feet; those pops dare them to look away from the screen at their peril; they will miss something truly interesting if they don't pay attention.

Natural sound pauses transmitting the experience at crucial intervals are the antidote to short attention spans.

Using Sound as a Transition

Every story with a beginning, middle, and end needs to go from Point B to Point C somewhere in its structure. The VJ can write a sentence making a transition, but it is far more effective to find a piece of natural sound or bite that will fluidly set up that section. In the hypothetical example about Joe Doe, four pieces of natural sound helped move the story forward: (1) pouring coffee helped introduce Joe as a character with some detail about his life, (2) the car engine starting set the scene for him leaving for work, (3) the cash register set the scene of him working, and (4) the convenience door slamming set up the climax in which Joe resolved to find one more job to pay his bills.

Despite its strength as a storytelling tool, natural sound deserves a word of caution. If the story is complex, research shows viewers might comprehend and remember the story more easily if it has a slower pace. Write longer stretches of narration and use fewer or longer pieces of natural sound to help the audience comprehend more.[8]

Otherwise, keep the narration short; use a standup to demonstrate something that can't be shown. Use a natural sound break for a second or two before beginning narration after a sound bite. That will allow the audience to reflect for an instant on what has been said. It also prepares them to hear another voice or for the next step in the story.

It's also possible to use a series of shots to build a natural sound sequence. Use the sound in unforeseen, unpredictable ways that contribute to the story's momentum. Use sound to illustrate themes in the story. Judicious natural sound pauses keep the story moving toward a dramatic finish. Always write to get to the next piece of sound as soon as possible and you will keep your audience engaged and wondering just what will happen next.

One other tip while adding sound, write the time codes from your log sheet for each bite or piece of natural sound used in the script. That will help later in the editing process.

Put Muscle on the Skeleton

If sound is the skeleton for the story, then the writing attaches muscle to the bones, or context and revealing detail that add richness to the story. What's the best way to make sure the muscle is well toned and not flabby?

There is only one rule that cannot be broken: be accurate. All the creativity in shooting, writing, and editing is for naught if the information is not correct. Being accurate starts with the reporting, getting the information correct in your notebook. Whether it is the pronunciation of an unusual name, the spelling of a city on a super, or the amount of the upcoming tax increase, *it's got to be right every time.*

Getting it wrong jeopardizes your credibility; getting it wrong more than a few times jeopardizes your job.

The corollary to being accurate is to be neutral. Don't editorialize, even innocuously, by saying things like, "Hopefully the workers will clean up the oil spill."

The writer/journalist hoping for something is editorializing. It may seem to be a universal sentiment, but get a source to say it instead of you. If you can justify it with the facts from your reporting, the better way to phrase the same idea would be: "The townspeople hope the workers will clean up the oil spill."

The rest of the writing tips are guidelines, ones that make the story easy to read and understand since the audience normally has just one chance to hear and see the story. The guidelines work most of the time, but there are occasions when violating them could make the story more compelling, richer, or easier to understand. The more you write, the better you will be able to tell whether violating the guidelines makes your story stronger or weaker.

First, write in the third person. The piece is not about the reporter, so avoid writing in the first person. Don't say, "I went to such and such to talk to so and so." It can also be more engaging for the audience to write some part in the second person. If you are doing a consumer story with tips, for example, then writing in the second person is appropriate: "You can save money on gas by making slow, smooth starts at stoplights."

Next, use complete sentences. Otherwise, it sounds as if a Neanderthal wrote it: Fire bad! Story weak. Not way talk. Save incomplete sentences for headlines.

Use short sentences. Don't confuse your listeners with long, compound, run-on sentences with a series of thoughts that defy comprehension. Simple is better: one thought per sentence will keep the story flowing with clarity.

Be an Active-Voice Writer!

Look for strong verbs that help paint a picture with your video. Avoid weak, wimpy forms of the verb to be: is, are, was, were. Yet also be realistic; those verbs may be the best and simplest way of communicating the idea you want to get across.

Normally write using the present tense to give the story more immediacy; even events that happened in the past may have effects that are current. If the city council voted to increase taxes five hours ago, it is still correct to say, "Get ready for another raid on your wallet. The city raises taxes again."

Also use the active voice. Active voice is when the subject acts on an object in the sentence. Structure it with the subject first, then the verb and an object. Active voice is clear and direct. Verbs expressed in the passive voice show something else acting on the subject, which is indirect and requires a longer sentence construction.

Find strong, active verbs and make a subject act on them to make it forceful. "The surf pounded the beach." Not: "The beach was pounded by the surf." The passive voice in the latter saps the strength of the sentence. Using the active voice instead of the wimpy passive voice will help keep the audience engaged in the story.

Don't confuse passive voice with past tense. Past tense is helpful in many cases. After all, most stories are about things that have happened already, rather than something happening at the exact moment or that will take place in the future. So make sure you know the difference between passive voice and past tense. Then use the active voice because it is a more forceful way of expressing an idea.

Active voice and past tense: George Washington slept here.

Passive voice and past tense: This bed was slept in by George Washington.

Active voice makes the writing clearer and more succinct. Using strong, forceful verbs in the active voice help the storyteller paint a picture with the video.

After a litany of active-voice verbs, however, slip in one that is passive. It will keep the writing from sounding too sing-song, giving the story a change-up from the barrage of short sentences with forceful verbs. One place where passive voice could be useful is if you are describing a victim, someone or something that had no control over what happened: the man was stabbed by the assailant; the town was struck by the tornado.

There are many occasions, too, when we don't know the subject of a sentence, in other words, who or what caused something to happen. In those cases passive voice will have to do: "The money was stolen at lunch time."

Cut the Waste

Avoid expressing ideas with negatives. Instead, find a similar way to say the same thing positively. Since your viewers have only once chance to understand what you are saying, using negatives creates a barrier to that by challenging them to understand two concepts at the same time. For example, "not easy" is a negative way of expressing an idea. Using the word "hard" is a better way to express the same concept. "Not easy" requires the listener to comprehend the meaning of easy and then in the same instant the opposite of the word. The positive way of expressing the same idea, "hard," is easier to understand because it is just one concept instead of two.

Be concise. Don't use two words when one will do. Avoid redundancy unless you are trying to make a point by using multiple words with similar meanings. Otherwise, the writing becomes flabby and less clear.

Other standard broadcast news writing techniques also apply:

If there is a difficult name to pronounce, write it phonetically in the script so you don't stumble while reading it. Do you say the city's name bo-go-TAH as in Colombia or buh-GO-tuh as in New Jersey?

If you need to put a fact in a story, attribute the source first and then give the information: "The FBI reports the nation's murder rate decreased last year."

When identifying someone in your copy, normally give their title before the name: "Fire chief Tim Bowers says the fire started in the basement."

Use the first and last names of a person on the first reference in the story. After that, if the person is a continuing character, the type of story will dictate how you should refer to them. If it is a feature about a child or someone you want the audience to bond with on a first-name basis, use the first name. For most stories, however, use the person's last name on continuing references in the story.

Use contractions in your copy. It is more conversational than the full words.

Make it easy to pronounce numbers when you read the script. Use words for the numbers one to ten and numerals (11–999) for the rest. For really big numbers, such as 142,568, use a combination of numerals and words: write "142 thousand 568."

Last, but certainly not least among the standard broadcast writing techniques, read your copy out loud. As you write a difficult sentence try it out aurally. You may have written "20 five-gallon containers" in the script. But people listening at home may hear "25 gallon containers." After completing the entire story, read all of it aloud to see how it flows from beginning to end.

Write Literately to the Pictures

The chapter opened with the idea that the VJ needs to write with a picture in mind. Writing to the pictures means people will understand the stories and remember the details better than if the words and pictures don't match.[9]

That doesn't mean you have to write "dog" whenever a dog appears in the picture. That is something people obviously see on the screen. KUSA-TV news director Patti Dennis says, "We talk here a lot about writing to the video, but I see so much of . . . 'police surrounded the house with tape,' so I can see that, why do you tell me? I can see that! Can't you write above the video?"[10]

To write above the video, say something from the facts or background that you have uncovered that *add* meaning and context to what appears in the video. In other words, don't write literally, write literately. Polish your video with well-crafted words.

Metaphors can be useful in painting word pictures with video. One vivid example comes from NBC's Bob Dotson, who, when covering a storm that struck several southeast communities, wrote, "The tornado fired point blank . . ." The metaphor created an image of the tornado as a weapon that took aim at several towns. This helped set up a story with a running theme in which the storm was a villain terrorizing its victims.

In that same story, Dotson used another useful writing trick, alliteration. He wrote the tornado "sucked the roof off a Sears store." The video showed only the aftermath of the destruction, but the strong verb planted an image of the

KUSA News Director Patti Dennis wants her reporters to "write above the video." That means adding context that viewers can't see for themselves in the video.

storm in action. Using "sucked" in combination with the other "S" words gave the story a literate cadence as well.[11]

Another standard writing trick is to use the "rule of threes." Arranging things in a series of three provides a verbal cadence that flows well off the tongue:

A, B, C . . .

Do, re, mi . . .

One, two, three . . .

Cables, keyboards, and compact disks are no longer essential in computing.

Besides providing a pleasant cadence, using three examples can help prove a point. This is especially true if you need to show the virtues or faults of a character. For example, if a person in the story has done one thing bad, folks will likely forgive it as an unfortunate mistake. If the person has done a couple of things wrong, yeah, he bears keeping an eye on, but he may not be all that bad. If you name three examples that the subject has done maliciously, then the character may rise to villainy in storytelling parlance. You've nailed the case with three egregious actions.

It's as simple as one, two, three; A, B, C; do, re, mi.

Surprise Me!

Creative writing in packages has its place, yet writers need to be careful not to overdo some writing techniques. The overuse or misplacement of alliteration may make the story weary. Another writing trick, puns, might also be fun and useful in the right spots, but be troublesome if deployed incorrectly.

There is one writing tool, however, that never seems to be overused. Surprises —sometimes called reveals or twists—help keep the audience guessing what will come next and, therefore, glued to the screen to see where the story is heading.

As mentioned in the section on writing leads, you never want to give the whole story away at the beginning. Instead, the writer should reveal it layer by layer, twist after twist, surprise by surprise, building to a bold climax.

Surprises can come in many forms. It could be a key fact revealed at just the right moment. It might be a sound bite in which a character mentions a new wrinkle in the set of developing circumstances. Or it could be a piece of natural sound that takes the story in an unexpected direction.

Here is a natural sound and narrated opening that set up a surprise in one of the author's packages:

> *Wide shot with nat/snd: Dixieland combo playing "Sweet Georgia Brown"*
> *Reporter: "The mood upbeat, the occasion festive, all for a couple of words that haven't been heard here in two decades."*
> *Nat/snd of man swinging a lantern: "All aboard . . ."*

That second short piece of natural sound revealed the direction of the package in a way that, if left to the reporter's narration, would have been mundane. Sure, the narration could have said the band was playing to welcome passengers to the train, but that would fail to write above the video. Use all the pieces of the story puzzle, natural sound, bites, narration, or standups to continually reveal surprises and keep the audience engaged.

Recreate the Mood

Another way to write above the video is to recreate the mood or feeling of an event, the ephemeral things viewers can see in a picture, but do not fully understand. A savvy reporter and writer can use telling details to add greater dimensions to the video. Capturing the environment in pictures and natural sound, finding a good character and writing to those can bring the experience and feeling of being on the scene home to the audience.

> *Nat/snd—medium shot, light rain falling over small trees in plastic containers*
> *Reporter: "A cloud fell over the Buckingham Nursery today."*
> *Nat/snd—close-up of tree clippers chopping down small tree*

This was the way the author opened a story about a retired marine who ran a citrus nursery in his backyard in Florida. Problem was, Mac McKinney had received trees that had been exposed to citrus canker from another grower. To protect the powerful citrus industry from the virulent disease, the state had the right to come into Mac's little operation and destroy every citrus tree he had.

Obviously, this was a bad day for Mac; the rainy day just added to his gloom. State workers whacking down innocent-looking trees, then stacking them in a pile illustrated the grave situation; natural sound of the raindrops' patter punctuated the despair. But the narration did not state the obvious: "Rain fell on Buckingham Nursery today." Instead the script developed the environment and the natural sound of the rain as a metaphor to set the tone for everything that happened after that. Every few sentences a sound bite from Mac bitterly protesting the state intrusion made viewers feel his pain. The *coup de grace* was McKinney proclaiming that the state agriculture commissioner didn't send along a check to pay for his loss.

The narration, "A cloud fell over the Buckingham Nursery," gave a human context to the two dimensions of pictures and sound. Writing to the natural sound and video accentuated the theme of gloom that continued throughout the story. The narration revealed that Mac was relying on the nursery for his retirement income and now it was gone until the state repaid him. At the end, the story came full circle with the idea that started the story. The camera began tight on Mac shaking his head in the rain then zoomed out as the state truck, loaded with his trees, pulled away in another cloudburst:
Reporter: "It's said in everyone's life a little rain must fall. Today Mac McKinney got his share."

This was a literate—rather than a literal—way to begin and end the story with a theme that gave it focus throughout the piece. The story had an empathetic character paired against an unfeeling bureaucracy trying to protect an industry important to the whole state; natural sound and bites transmitted the experience of being there; the writing set up the full-circle theme and added facts that gave the story context of how one man's misfortune fit into the big picture of protecting Florida's agricultural economy.

Write a strong opening with natural sound and words that set up the ideas you wish to build on throughout the rest of the piece. Build your words, video, and sound to make sure you have a strong close. The ending is the place where you will have maximum impact on your audience, where you want them to shed a tear or flash a smile over something they felt through a well-told story.

Don't just end the story abruptly. Use every piece of the puzzle to close with a big finish.

Clear Your Mind and Take a Fresh Look at Your Work

Great writing usually doesn't happen when you first sit down at the keyboard or notepad to craft the story. Write your first draft, then take a break. Get away from the story on deadline for five or ten minutes and come back to it. Getting away from the story for a while, clearing your mind, will allow you to come back to it with a fresh perspective.

Polish the lead and ending.

See if the natural sound transitions work the way you thought they did.

Get rid of redundant verbiage.

If you are working on a story that has a longer deadline, write it one day and sleep on it overnight. Come back to do the second draft with renewed vigor and a clearer eye for detail. Sleep on it again and rework succeeding drafts to sharpen an already well-honed tale.

Before editing the story, always have someone review your writing. No matter how good the writer, often times tunnel vision sets in that blinds them to errors. Another set of eyes can spot inconsistencies, factual errors, inadvertent grammar problems, and other mistakes that might ruin the story. A good editor can spot those mistakes to help make a well-told story even better.

As you are writing to get to the next piece of sound, this is the time where your vision begins to come alive. Focus on creating a well-told story, one that features useful information, intriguing characters, plus engaging video and sound.

Discussion and VJ Exercise

1. Take the video you shot and logged from the exercise in chapter 4. Choose a good opening shot with natural sound, two to three good pieces of natural sound that will work for the middle part of the story and a good closing shot.

2. Now write a story from your log sheet and notes using the techniques described in this chapter. Use natural sound to make transitions that flow from one point of the story to the next. How can you write "above the video" in the opening and closing?

3. After getting away from your script overnight, come back and rewrite it with a fresh eye to improve the opening and closing sequences. Also review the writing and natural sound breaks: make sure that the script uses active voice and that the natural sound breaks flow easily from segment to segment.

4. Have a colleague review your script for accuracy and to make sure it is a well-told story from beginning, middle, to end. Offer to review your colleague's writing as well. Learn from each other's mistakes and techniques.

5. Look at a newspaper story that is written in a typical print style. Rewrite it in broadcast style paying attention especially to using present tense and active voice.

Chapter 7 Focus
Use a Log Sheet to Find Pieces of the Story Puzzle

Logging your video is critical to finding the best pieces to assemble your story puzzle. It is a time-consuming, mundane chore, but gives the VJ a full awareness of the nuances and moments that she or he shot while in the field.

Over a two-year period the author shot video for a documentary, *Heritage or Hate?* This is a partial log sheet from one tape that the author used several months later to write the script for the documentary. Places with underlines are to emphasize bites or natural sound to make them easy to find later.

You can use this as model for your own log sheets, or develop your own system of logging. The important thing is to log your video before writing your story.

TAPE #12
0:00:47 WS (from outside fence) looking toward city of Elmwood cemetery
    from same spot as summer/this time no flag or pole
0:01:53 MS of top of monument and no flag pole
0:02:24 CU of plaque on ground and mini flag
0:02:52 WS with fence in foreground of cemetery/monument/gravestones
0:03:59 zoom out from mini flag to WS of fence ends at 0:04:19
0:4:57 zoom in from ws to mini flag ends 5:17
0:05:17 low angle of monument with flag etched in stone
0:06:00 CU patch of concrete where flag pole stood (leaf falls on concrete)
0:06:32 MS of concrete and tombstones behind
0:07:13 nat/.snd (wind and leaves blow through shot)
0:07:32 CU of tombstone man killed in 1862
0:08:44–:56 zoom out from 1862 tombstone to concrete flag pole patch
then zoom in 9:14–9:22 redo zoom out at 9:47–9:57—better
0:10:16 CU mini flag in grass with tombstones behind
0:10:45 ws of same
0:11:05 CU of mini flag in ground at base of monument
SCV protest on street
0:13:24 WS from side of protestors

0:13:53 ms protestors through trees from side . . . see flags better

0:14:22 WS from across street 14:46 cars passing possible nat/snd

0:14:59 ms from across street of protestors (American flag in the background)

0:15:17 ms—van passes through shot obscures flags momentarily—again

0:15:44—wider shot

0:15:52 from above across street . . . looking through trees at protestors

interview <u>David Mullis</u> Rockhill, SC 803-448-4392 VIDEO A BIT HOT

0:16:55 Unfortunately this flag's been associated with the Klan. Even though they did use it, we in no way, shape or form support them. 17:03

0:17:28 Most of the African Americans want us to be able to honor our ances-tors. 17:36 There's a small group of people who have moved here from other parts of the country and are offended by the flag probably because they're just not educated by the flag 17:44 and the confederacy 17:45

0:18:27 hopefully get the flag back up there just by raising awareness 18:31 and letting people know it has nothing to do with racism whatsoever, it's all about honoring our ancestors. 18:35

0:19:42 I can't think of any place that is more fitting than the confederate sec-tion of a cemetery for that flag to fly 19:49 uh, <u>I can understand it having to come off a state owned or city owned building 19:55, but we're talking about a Confederate gravesite here. 19:57 uh it's no different than if Normandy, France said oh somebody over here's offended by the American flag flying over Normandy 20:04 It's gotta come down. It's the same thing, it just makes absolutely no sense. 20:08</u>

0:21:05 As members of the Sons of Confederate Veterans we're charged with upholding the Confederate soldiers' good name no matter if it's a relative or not. 21:13

0:21:25 ~~And everybody who is buried there did die during the war and they are from all states. They're not just from North Carolina~~ NOT TRUE . . . I SAW SOME WHO DIED AFTER THE WAR.

INTERVIEW   CLAUDE HEFNER   Charlotte resident

VIDEO IS HOT

WHAT DOES REMOVING FLAG FROM CEMETERY MEAN TO HIM?

0:23:21 It means a colossal slap in the face

0:23:23 They'll allow any flag (waves finger and hand) to fly until the Confed-erate flag goes up and one whine from the NAACP and the vote pandering begins. 23:36 That's the root of the whole thing. 23:38 (SOME OF THIS IS GOING ON BEFORE CITY CAMPAIGN SEASON)

0:24:50 ws of groups standing with flags

25:42 low angle looking up at man holding flag

0:25:50 men standing holding flags MS

0:25:57 WS men holding flags

Denne Sweeney interview

About cemetery

0:26:50 These guys are pretty determined and this is a pretty basic issue with them taking down a flag over a confederate cemetery. I mean it doesn't get any more basic than that. 26:59

from one to ten on heritage violations?

0:27:08 It's about nine and three quarters. It's pretty high. 27:12 I think the only thing they could do worse than this is threaten to take down the grave stones, 27:14 which they've also threatened to do in some locations. 27:17

higher heritage violation than SC capitol issue   why?

0:28:06 <u>We're talking about actual graves of our ancestors. This is what the SCV is all about, protecting the reputation of our Confederate ancestors. 28:16 I mean these were honorable men who fought for an honorable cause and what's more basic than flying a flag over their graves? 28:22</u>

28:33 These are veterans and they need to be honored in their way too.

28:37 about SCV shake-up   no other organization allows all the past officers to have a vote . . . doesn't expect any policy change as a result . . . focusing on heritage violations is still his main concern

0:29:46 The main question is who's going to do that? Who's going to control that? 29:50 The past commanders in chief and their supporters basically think the elected officials shouldn't have any say in this. They're the old group that thinks they should continue to run things forever. 30:02

0:31:22 low angle looking up . . . men walking by with flags

<u>vigil at Elmwood Cemetery</u>

35:50 WS of cty

36:06 ws men gathering in distance with tombstones foreground

36:18 MS of men, with two flags prominent

36:28 murmur as CU of lighting candles—shows woman shielding flame from breeze <u>GOOD SHOT TO OPEN SEQUENCE</u> goes to 36:33

36:54—one man lighting candle from another

37:15 man and woman standing with Georgia flag and shielding candles

38:03 CU candle, pan up to see <u>Claude Hefner</u> . . . and flag goes by behind him to 38:15

38:35 people walking to monument

38:55 following HEFNER carrying flag and candle and walking to monument to 39:14 MIGHT ALSO BE GOOD OPENING SHOT FOR SEQUENCE (use under his bite above???)

39:16 ECU of candle

MAN . . . NOT IDd , believe first name is Dennis (dark-framed between two flags) 39:47 We're here to honor our ancestors who fought for their homes, who fought for their way of life. 39:54

40:19—cu of candle zoom out to people

40:48—kick in gain

40:53 MS—shows men with candles and flags

41:15 WS of group and flags

00:41:54 EWS from behind monument with tombstones foreground

singing Dixie quietly,,, capture sound while walking 42:17 In Dixieland I'll take
my stand to live and die in Dixie 42:23 away, away, away down south in Dixie
42:28 away, away, away down south in Dixie 42:37

Chapter 8

The Vision Comes Alive

Whether the video story will be on air or online, the VJ still must edit it. This can be both a challenging and exhilarating part of the storytelling experience. This is the place where the VJ's vision becomes apparent for all to see.

Just as the shooting required the VJ to master a number of technical details, editing requires the VJ to be proficient in a specialized area as well. Whether one is using Final Cut Pro, one of the Avid editing software products, Pinnacle, or a variety of other nonlinear computer editors—or even editing on tape—each product has similarities and differences.

Whatever system you use, a couple of tips could help organize the work and save time when editing. First, use time codes from your log sheet and script to capture only the clips you need rather than all of the video that you shot. Then save the clips into bins, such as BITES or NAT/SND, with descriptive file names that will help you find them when you are ready to use them.

The more you use your preferred or company-specified editing solution, the better you will be; as you gain more experience you will be able to step out of the novice mode, barely slamming a story together on deadline, and be able to put more creative touches into your final edited story with ease.

Give the Story Meaning with Your Voice

If you've decided to write the story instead of produce a natural sound package, now you have to read it or, more accurately, read it out loud for the audience. The trick to voicing a good story is to sound as if you aren't reading at all. Yet you must make sure you have the proper announcing technique to make the story interesting enough to hold the audience's attention.

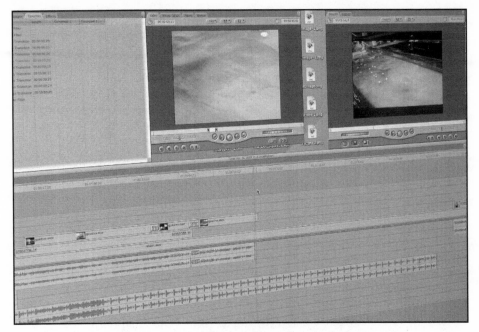

The nonlinear timeline is the place where the
VJ's vision begins coming together for all to see.

It's time to bring in that buddy who's having a beer with you again. Or maybe it's your mother or favorite uncle. Think of the people you want to tell the story to and then just talk to them. But now when you are talking about the story, you have to convey meaning to what you have written through your voice.

This is especially important if viewers will be watching your video on a more intimate screen than viewing a TV across the room. "Viewers want a delivery that feels like the person is having a latte with them at Starbucks," write Dave Cupp, a former TV news director, and Dr. Ann Utterback, a voice expert. "They are, after all, often holding that person in their hand as they watch on their iPhone or Blackberry."[1]

In those situations, you wouldn't talk in a monotone to your mother, buddy, or uncle while telling them a story. That would be boring. So don't do it when reading from your script either.

Vary the pitch in your voice. High-pitched voices sound less authoritative; if you have a normally high-sounding voice, try to bring it down to give yourself more credibility. Even if you normally have a lower tone, alter it: sometimes it should be higher; sometimes it should be lower, depending on how you want to interpret what you've written.

Also vary the inflection. That is the emphasis to give to each word. Some people underline certain words in the script that they want to highlight while voicing it. Doing that makes it more likely you will emphasize them and give the proper meaning to each sentence as you record the narration.

The pacing is also important. There may be times when the story should move a bit faster. Other times it should be slower to reflect the gravitas of the event.

Voice It with Appropriate Energy

Much of the announcing for your story comes down to the energy you put into the voicing. If you don't show that you are interested in the story through appropriate energy, the audience may be unimpressed and tune out.

What is appropriate energy? Imagine you are doing a story about a new video game that is taking the gaming community by storm; it has breakthrough graphics, sound that inserts users into the middle of the action, and a storyline that keeps them glued for hours. Wow! That will be a high-energy story that requires voicing that, if not excited, at least is animated.

On the other hand, the story on a funeral of a soldier killed in the war on terrorism would require a sober, slower-paced, low-intensity reading.

Most announcers stand when they read their copy since it improves the flow of air to and from the lungs. But announcers can also get good results sitting down as long as they breathe well by sitting up straight with their feet on the floor. "If you're slumping in a chair or pressing your back against the chair, it will inhibit this full breathing," writes voice expert Utterback.[2]

To get in the proper frame of mind for announcing a story, some reporters use their hands to gesture while reading. It helps them get in the mood, as if they are telling a friend about what they discovered while covering the story. When he first started as a VJ, former photographer Jerry Barlar of WKRN in Nashville found that if he put his hands in his pockets while reading, it made him more relaxed and allowed him to voice his scripts as if he were talking to a neighbor.[3]

To help your work stand out, find a way to develop your own voice when announcing. For new VJs, it may sound awkward at first to play back the audio and hear yourself. At first you may say, "That doesn't sound like me." But after a while you will get used to your own recorded voice. To get to that point, practice constantly. Read newspapers or magazines aloud using various techniques on the same sentences to see how they sound with different pacing, inflection, and pitch.

Unless you plan to do nothing but natural sound video essays, you need to get comfortable with your voice so your audience will be comfortable with it as well.

The Vision Comes Alive

All the hard work of reporting, shooting, logging, writing, and announcing now comes down to the final step, making your vision come alive by editing the video. As you wrote the story, you should already have had a compelling opening and dramatic closing shot in mind. Start editing with that opening shot and natural sound. After that, everything else should begin to fall in place as you follow your script and consult your log sheet to add narration, natural sound, video, and bites to the nonlinear editor's timeline.

One basic editing concept is to maintain continuity, which is a sequencing of shots that match the action as someone would view it. The sequence might go from wide shot to medium shot to close-up. Or it might as easily go from a close-up to the wide shot and to a medium shot. For example, the editor would cut from a wide shot of a person holding a telephone to a medium shot of the same person holding the phone. Note, however, that the person must be holding the phone in the same hand and to the same ear; otherwise, the shot would be a jump cut, which would leave the audience wondering how the phone switched positions—a distraction that would keep viewers from paying attention to the story's message.

Learning how to edit takes patience. But persistent
practice pays off with better and better stories.

Another way to maintain continuity is to use the technique of into and out of frame (how to shoot it is covered in chapter 6). In that same example of the telephone, the third shot in the sequence could be a close-up of the telephone's cradle as the hand gripping the phone comes into the frame to place the phone back in its resting spot.

This is another way the VJ might cut the sequence with an into and out frame shot:

1. Start with a close-up of a ringing telephone in its cradle. As the phone continues to ring, the close up shot shows a hand picking it up and then going out of frame.
2. The next shot is a wide shot of the person holding the telephone to her left ear.
3. The third shot in the sequence is a medium shot, or perhaps another close-up of the woman holding the telephone to her left ear.

Make Magic Come Alive

Using sequences, such as the one described above, helps the story flow; cutting sequential shots moves the story forward at a logical pace. Using video that has action, or movement of some kind, instead of static shots is another way to improve the pacing. "One of the things I and most every newspaper shooter needs to learn is how to edit for pacing," says Colin Mulvany, the multimedia editor for the *Spokesman-Review* in Spokane. "Many of our stories wander around, never getting to the point. We fail to edit in the little magic moments and surprises that keep a viewer staying to the end of our masterpieces."[4]

If you have logged the tape, you know where all those magic moments are. If you have written the story with pictures in mind for each sentence and to get to the next piece of sound as soon as possible, you have already edited the story in your mind. Now it's just a matter of pushing the right buttons to reveal your vision to others.

KGO-TV's Wayne Freedman admits that as a former TV photographer who got his start shooting and editing tape, one of the hardest parts of becoming a VJ was learning how to use the station's nonlinear editing software. His third VJ piece took him thirteen hours to edit, but was a breakthrough experience that made it easier—and him a better editor—on succeeding stories.[5]

The more you do video editing the more accomplished you will become. "It's a long process," says *washingtonpost.com* VJ Ben de la Cruz. "I don't think it's something you learn in like a month, say. It's an ongoing process."[6]

Editing practice is essential to becoming proficient. If you perform the editing well, people will be paying attention to the story instead of the editing techniques.

The rhythm of each story will be different. Using the example cited earlier, the soldier's funeral would be slower paced with fewer shots, while the rhythm of the video game piece would be full of action, a multitude of sound bites and natural sound breaks with cuts every few seconds. Each would require a different style of editing, yet there are techniques that will make each story stronger.

Don't Bounce from Scene to Scene

Stay in sequences as long as possible. You shot the sequences—wide shot, medium shot, close up—for a reason. If you cut too quickly from scene to scene, it will be a jumble of incomprehensible video that will confuse viewers. So set up a scene with a wide shot or close-up, then stay with other shots within the same sequence—such as reaction shots—until the storyline shifts to something that lends itself to a different scene.

The main editing technique to use is the cut, a simple change from one shot to the next. If you shot sequences and cutaways, you won't need dissolves or other effects to get from one point in the story to another. Peoples' eyes don't dissolve from scene to scene, but they do focus on something wide then narrow the focus to inspect it a bit closer. That is what a sequence of cuts can do. Save the dissolves and other effects for transitions from one sequence to another or to avoid a jarring jump cut.

In fact, a simple, well-told video story using mostly straight cuts is usually more effective than loading it up with effects. Research shows that music, sound effects, slow motion, and flash frames make a story less enjoyable, less informative, and less believable for viewers.[7]

Get into the Rhythm of the Story

The longer one edits, the more the editor gets a feel about what the proper length of a shot should be. Are there long stretches of narration with long sound bites, or does the story move swiftly with a lot of natural sound breaks and short sentences? Generally cut a shot to match the pacing and rhythm of the narration. That may mean cutting a shot for each sentence, but it is also possible to cut shots at pauses or breaks within a sentence. Occasionally, however, one shot may stretch into the next or even a third sentence. That will slow down the pacing and allow viewers more time to absorb information.

It's also good to vary the pacing of shots in the story; in other words, don't make every shot five seconds or eight seconds long. Variety will help keep the audience tuned in.

Don't cut in the middle of a zoom, a pan, or other camera movement. Edit a pan before the camera starts to move and end it after the camera stops. If it is a long camera movement, this is another way to slow down the pacing and let people absorb what they've been hearing and seeing.

More Sound Advice

The pace of the story should adhere to the writing, always getting to the next piece of sound—whether a sound bite or a natural sound break. That will make for a faster pace and help keep the audience's attention from slipping away.

One smooth way to edit sound in a story is to overlap it with another scene. For example, as one segment of narration ends, start the audio from a sound bite, but cover a few seconds of the bite with the video that closes the narration. This makes a natural way to move into a new segment of the story. People are used to hearing things without seeing them. They may be busy looking away from someone as they address them, then turn to look to see the source of the sound. Using the sound overlap technique mimics that natural occurrence.

A standard editing technique for reporter-voiced packages is to have the narration and sound bites on the timeline's first audio channel, with the natural sound under on the second channel. The VJ can use extra audio channels for music or to increase the sound level by copying it to other channels if the sound on one of the first two channels is too low.

Be critical of the sound levels. "Anything having to do with sound is what is going to make your edit better," says NPPA award-winning editor Greg T. Johnson of WFAA-TV in Dallas. "Sound is pretty much the most important thing in the edit. That pretty much makes or breaks the edit process."[8]

Make the sound levels smooth throughout the entire story, with nothing on the audio channels too high or too low. You can use either a software mixer to control a whole segment or key frames to put spots on the audio timeline. Adjusting those key frames higher or lower gives the editor infinite control of the sound in and out of sound bites and natural sound breaks. If used properly, the key frame technique (sometimes called "rubber banding") ends up looking like an economic graph with the line heading up and down the chart as the sound rises and falls.

Sound is so important that it should be underneath each shot in the narration. If there is some noise in a natural sound segment that is distracting from the story, either lower it so that it doesn't interfere with the narration or find some sound from the same scene that you shot that is not distracting and lay that in separately on the timeline.

Be aware, however, that some journalists frown at this last technique as an ethical lapse: the sound is not a *true* match with the video so it is not a picture of reality that journalism is supposed to show. The RTDNA Code of Ethics says journalists should neither manipulate sound or images in any way that is misleading nor reenact them without informing the audience.[9] Use your best judgment to determine whether the audio change is significant enough to alter the reality of the story or if the change is merely a minor enhancement that will not hinder the substance.

There are legitimate ways of cleaning up other sound issues. Using dissolves on the audio edits may help eliminate pops or sudden changes in the video levels. "I don't want to hear the edit. I want it to be seamless," says WFAA's Johnson.[10]

Use Effects Judiciously

Nonlinear editing also allows the VJ to use all sorts of effects to jazz up the video. You might use a one-frame still shot to let the viewer focus on a single shot without any movement; you can also use that with text over it to highlight critical information as well. You might also superimpose one shot over another, create a double box, or do a series of wipes in a sequence to make it stand out. Be very judicious, however, in whether these effects are necessary to tell the story. Sometimes just good video and sound are all one needs to tell a compelling story.

To Narrate? Or Not to Narrate?

Sometimes video storytellers don't write or narrate their story; instead, they merely open the editing program and assemble the video, natural sound, and sound bites in a coherent way to let the subjects of a story carry the message without any narration.

Producing a non-narrated, or natural sound, package requires mostly organizational skills that can bring the beginning, middle, and end of the story to life without the context that writing can provide. This is the case not only for video essays for television news, but also for newspaper VJs doing non-narrated mini-documentaries.

"I feel like there's a little more freedom to kind of do things differently [than in TV news]," says former *washingtonpost.com* VJ Pierre Kattar. Unlike TV reporters, the decision to narrate is not automatic for Kattar. He says there is no set pattern to help determine whether he will do a story with or without narration. "When I decide to narrate, I just want to do it as minimally as possible. I don't feel my voice has any place in the piece."[11]

The stories that most often can be told without narration, says the VJ are those that are personality driven, pieces about just one person. Kattar says the stories that need narration—or a text slide to provide the same information—are those that need more context than sound bites and natural sound alone can provide. Complex topics may need text or narration to provide that background. Sometimes, too, interviewees say something the VJ did not capture on camera, but is worthy enough to include in the story, so that may also require the VJ to write narration for the story.[12]

Editing Non-narrated Video Stories

At the *New York Times,* Ann Derry, the editorial director of video, says, "Most often, the reporting is complicated and nuanced enough that we need to use voiceover narration to add context and information to the piece. In *Times* videos, the narrator is almost always the reporter or the video journalist who produced the story."[13]

If your story is to be a mini-documentary or video essay with no narration, however, the story will have to stand alone from beginning to middle to the end. It may help, however, to outline—actually write out—the order of the puzzle pieces of sound bites and natural sound before beginning to edit to make sure they make sense and build a complete story from start to finish.

Some editors working on a non-narrated story, however, just assemble the pieces without a script, using the nonlinear editing system to add, subtract, or reconstruct from the timeline to make sense of the story as they go along. Multimedia journalist and educator Richard Koci Hernandez writes, "My workflow includes producing the audio narrative FIRST, then letting the other layers support my audio narrative."[14]

Former *washingtonpost.com* VJ Kattar follows the same procedure when editing a non-narrated piece: "First I just get down the interview with the person and see if it makes sense."[15]

Angela Grant's specialty is editing nonnarrated, natural-sound stories.

When doing this type of story, it's often best to let interviewees introduce themselves as they reveal themselves as characters and what they have to do with the story. If the story needs more information than bites and natural sound alone can provide, then the VJ may need to add text slides or other graphics to make sure the audience has the context to understand the full story.

Other Web Editing Tricks

A video story for the Web will also be different from one edited for television in other ways. The Web story may be longer and use more natural sound than can be used in the traditional minute-and-a-half TV story. Yet there are limits that the audience will endure. "We like to keep our videos between three and five minutes," writes the *Times*'s Derry. "That seems to be the sweet spot, and not just in terms of holding viewers' attention: It's the time it takes to tell many of our video stories."[16]

Part of the editing process for the Web may also require the VJ to find and upload a great still photo or graphic on the opening page to grab attention in addition to writing a line or two setting up the video. The VJ might also decide to break the story into different parts to make them shorter and more interactive for the online audience. If it is a multimedia project and the VJ is Flash-literate, he or she may also want to build elements that complement the video with that tool. A word of caution, however, from *New York Times* chief multimedia producer Gabriel Dance. He says don't overuse flashy tricks at the expense of the content: "People aren't there to play with your buttons, they're not there to figure out your cool navigation system. They're there to see your photographs. Or they're there to see the video."[17]

Also, unlike TV news, which normally puts supers on the stories while the newscast is on the air live, the VJ will have to edit any supers and other graphics into the story's timeline for a Web story. And, of course, the VJ will have to export the story in whatever format is required to view it on the organization's Web site.

Make a Final Review

Whether doing a narrated or non-narrated piece, once all the video and sound are down, take a view minutes to critically review what you have edited. Pay special attention to the opening to make sure it grabs viewers' attention and the close leaves them with a tear or a smile. Make sure the sound levels are even throughout; eliminate flash frames; make sure the length of each shot is just right. There may never be a "perfect" story, but this is your last chance to make sure it has the impact you want.

Then if you don't have an immediate deadline bearing down on you, before publishing it to the Web or sending it to air, show it to a colleague for feedback.

After showing a story to someone, VJ Roger M. Richards makes a point of asking them how long it ran. He says if they say it is shorter than the actual time, he thinks he did a good job of making the story flow.[18]

There are all kinds of puzzle pieces a VJ can manipulate to write and edit a compelling story that will constantly engage the audience. The vision begins with a story idea, but after reporting, shooting, and writing, it finally comes to life little by little, edit by edit for everyone to see.

Discussion and VJ Exercise

1. Take the story you wrote in the chapter 7 exercise and record narration for it. Practice reading it with different inflection, emphasis, and pacing. Read it once as if it were a story for a funeral. Read it again as if it were a story about the hometown team winning a national championship. Is either approach good for your actual story? Or should it be a blend of the two?

2. Review the techniques you use for your nonlinear editing software and any specific technical specifications your organization requires for an edited video story. Do you know how to capture video with sound? Do you know how to edit sound alone to one channel of audio? Do you know how to get video and audio to one channel of the timeline without getting the sound on the other channels? Do you know how to move sound from one channel of the source video to a different channel on the timeline? Can you create and edit supers into the timeline? If the answer is no to any of the above questions, then practice the technique until you can do it flawlessly on a deadline.

3. Edit the narrated story you wrote from chapter 7 on your nonlinear editor using the techniques described in this chapter.

4. What is your view of changing sound under a shot if the sound is bad or distracting? Is it ethical or unethical? Is using video effects, such as a dissolve, also unethical?

5. View Joe Little's standups on YouTube at: www.youtube.com/watch ?v=TO356cp9tKE&eurl=http://www.b-roll.net/forum/showthread. php?t=22796. After viewing the standups, discuss the techniques he uses to produce them. Can you duplicate his techniques? If not, what do you need to learn to do them?

Chapter 8 Focus
When and How to Do Standups

On the nontechnical side of the VJ equation, doing standups is one of the toughest parts of the assignment. Not every story requires a standup. Often a well-crafted story needs only video, natural sound, and characters to speak for themselves. At other times narration, along with a standup, may be necessary to tie all the elements together. If a standup is needed or required by the news organization, it is usually the first part of the story the VJ has to write; it often has to be shot before all of the pieces of the story come together.

As a result, the VJ may not have a good sense of what the standup should say. So, the first thing the solo videojournalist needs to create an effective standup is a mental outline of what the entire story will look like and how the standup will fit into that piece. If the story is still unfolding with an uncertain outcome by the deadline, the VJ may find it necessary to shoot two or more versions of the standup.

Some news organizations require their reporters to do "look lives," which are not live at all, but instead are recorded standups at the beginning and end of a package. A look live requires a solid on-camera introduction and wrap-up to pull it off, but otherwise doesn't lend itself to creative video storytelling. The bookend standups should not be called a live shot or have a graphic indicating that it is.

So, unless the VJ is doing a look live, the best place to incorporate a standup is as a bridge in the middle of the story. It is better to start the story with compelling video and natural sound; it is more effective to wrap up by coming full circle with a reminder of how the story started—and that is not a standup.

Making a transition from one point in the story to another, or as a way to illustrate something that otherwise can't be shown on camera, is a good way to use a standup. The VJ can use the standup to provide context or background for the story. These techniques, of course, work best somewhere in the middle of the story.

The standup should be part of a seamless flow from one part of the story to another. Don't bring the flow to a halt by needlessly inserting a reporter when other elements can be used to tell the story better. Rather than just telling the audience something, use the standup to demonstrate a concept, show them something that a sound bite could not or that is difficult or impossible to illustrate with video. But don't force the demonstration if it doesn't work naturally. The standup should have a natural motivation that works well with the theme in the story.

There are a couple of different methods for actually delivering a standup. When the VJ recites the words, it could be memorized or delivered with a more off-the-cuff style. The first will convey exactly what the VJ wants to say, but may sound stiff. The second, using an outline highlighting key words rather than memorizing the script, may have varied content from take to take, but may sound more conversational and natural.

It is not necessary in either case for the VJ to maintain eye contact with the lens throughout the standup. It is natural when talking to someone to look away from time to time. This is especially useful if the VJ is demonstrating something; it will seem normal to look at the object being demonstrated for a few seconds and then back at the camera.

Technically, it is more difficult for a VJ to shoot a standup than it is for two people to perform the same task. Yet one-man bands using tripods have mastered the art of doing standups for years. For a simple standup, you can place something on the ground where you will stand and focus the camera on that. To get a more exact focus, erect a light stand where you want to be in the standup. Raise the stand to the top of your head, put one of the lock-down knobs where your nose would be, then focus and frame on that. When you are ready to shoot, just move the light stand out of the way and roll.

On a camera with a maneuverable viewfinder, the VJ can also tilt it forward to judge accurate framing and monitor what is happening behind her while shooting.

Dan Adams utilizes a reversible viewfinder on his camera to frame his standups.

Some VJs have found more creative ways of doing standups. Joe Little, a digital correspondent at KGTV in San Diego, injects personality and multiple takes as well as some editing tricks into his stories to make his standups outshine many reporters who work in two-person crews.

Here are three of Little's techniques: (1) he frames something in the foreground on a wide shot then walks into frame at an unusual angle to talk in the background; (2) he rides a bike from the background to the foreground, reciting his standup while his image continually grows larger in the frame; (3) he uses multiple cuts on a single camera set-up and then edits it to make it appear as if he is in two places at once.[1]

Even though she doesn't always use one, Heidi McGuire at KUSA in Denver has earned a reputation for doing solo standups that leave her colleagues quizzing, "How did she do that?"

"I've taken up to an hour of my time to shoot a 5-part standup," says McGuire. But she also says she needs to make sure the time she spends doing that has a good payoff in the story itself. "The fun for me is people think you can't do it, but oh, you can!"[2]

Some VJs have discovered ways to actually move the camera while doing a standup. "If you've got a pan handle just below the camera," says BBC solo videojournalist Tom Hepworth, "you can do a cheeky little pan." On some cameras, he suggests VJs can pre-program the menu so that it zooms out or in to add visual interest to the standup. "I would say that's probably the trickiest thing you do as a VJ," he adds.[3]

If you are demonstrating something in the standup, shoot the wide shot first. Deliver the information flawlessly without stumbles or unnecessary pauses. Check it out by replaying it to make sure the sound is okay, the framing is positioned as you want it. Then, shoot a cut-in, a close-up of the item you want to demonstrate. This time, zoom in to where you held the demonstrated item at the same position in the wide shot. Shoot the close-up as you pick up the item or move it into the spot you want in the frame.

Once again, check the video to make sure the cut-in will work with the wide shot part of the standup. Later you can edit a sequence as the item comes into frame, or as a close-up after it has already moved. This will make a nicely matched action shot rather than just a static wide shot for your standup.

Chapter 9

Not Your Father's Video Story

It's a golden idol. The winged female statuette reaches skyward raising a symbolic globe over her head. This is an Emmy statue, one which the best TV news operations around the country have been honored to receive.

But this Emmy award rests not in a case at some TV station or broadcast network, but on a counter at a snack bar at the *Washington Post's* Web and multimedia operation center. In fact, *washingtonpost.com* has won multiple local and national Emmys. The newspaper also has won *video* awards from the White House Press Photographers Association and even Murrow awards from the Radio Television News Director's Association (now the Radio Television Digital News Association). Not to be outdone, the *New York Times* also boasts several video prizes, including duPont-Columbia and Peabody awards.[1]

Setting Themselves Apart from TV News

These are not your father's newspapers. Nor is the video produced the kind that your father grew up watching on television. Video stories produced at *washingtonpost.com* and other newspapers around the country are not only changing the way viewers receive video, but redefining what videojournalism is all about.

"When I got here we had one little VHS camcorder, one VHS deck, one capture card, and nobody knew how to do anything," says Chet Rhodes, the deputy multimedia editor and chief trainer for print reporters morphing into video storytellers.[2]

That was in 1998. A year later Travis Fox arrived to work as a photo editor. He soon found that single VHS camera and started using it. "1999 was a good

One sure sign that newspapers are making inroads into TV's once sacrosanct video genre is these Emmys won by *washingtonpost.com*.

time to learn Web video, because no one was watching, not even my own editors," he says. "In fact, I had to sneak around to do video because the bandwidth was so big and the technology was so bad that a couple of times our editor would try to watch the video and crash the computer and call I.T. in."[3]

Yet before he was laid off in 2009,[4] Fox became one of the top VJs at *washingtonpost.com*, traveling the world to shoot and report stories on his own and winning Emmys and video awards from the White House Press Photographers Association and teaching videojournalism seminars for the National Press Photographers Association.

Managers at *washingtonpost.com* and the newspaper itself took greater notice of his work when he began turning out video stories on the war in Iraq that were competitive with other news organizations. "I think my style in general is different from some parts of television but not all. It's not reporter driven and it's not celebrity-anchor driven," said Fox. "That's not to say that it's not heavily reported and heavily narrated because a lot of them are. I would say the ones we did in the beginning were more different from television—they were more character-driven pieces, less narration."[5]

Others followed in Fox's footsteps. Before a recession-related downsizing, there was a stable of six VJs at *washingtonpost.com*; even the newspaper's reporters got in the habit of picking up small video cameras to shoot interviews and video to post on the Web site.

Newspapers Add More Video to the Mix

The *Washington Post* may have been among the first newspapers to start using video on the Web, but as the video gathering and editing equipment got cheaper, and people started getting their daily dose of information from the Web, newspapers and magazines around the country began rushing to add video to their mix of journalism products.

"The walls are being broken down between broadcast and print journalists," wrote Society of Professional Journalists president Clint Brewer, who is the executive editor of *The City Paper* in Nashville. "Increasingly, the tag of being an 'online' journalist is also fading, as all journalists become online journalists."[6]

A survey in late 2007 by a Massachusetts digital media buyer, Burst Media, found that 44 percent of those viewing Web video liked news clips the best and nearly 59 percent of people sixty-five years and older had seen an online video.[7]

When cruising newspaper and magazine Web sites, a viewer can discover a wealth of video commentaries from established print reporters, coverage of breaking news events, and mini-documentaries. Much of it is done by solo videojournalists aiming to make their mark in this new media world. "We are reinventing journalism," says the *New York Times* video editorial director Ann Derry.[8]

Before it went on the auction block, *Newsweek,* a *Washington Post* subsidiary, hired four video producers who shoot and edit their own video. The company did not rely on TV news professionals, however, but young, creative, Web-savvy journalists. "The technologies that they work with," says *Newsweek.com* editor Diedre Depke, "are so completely different from television that we think that was the way to go."[9]

Indeed, finding a traditional print medium these days that does not use video on its Web site is a tough challenge. The *Modesto Bee,*[10] the *Louisville Courier-Journal,*[11] and the *Chicago Tribune*[12] are among those that have shifted duties of traditional print photographers to news videographers. The *Detroit Free Press* used twenty-five people to produce an Emmy award-winning documentary on Aretha Franklin. The paper's digital media managing editor, Nancy Andrews, says, "We start with the premise that we're storytellers, with strong visuals and a compelling story to begin with."[13]

Here Come the MoJos

In Florida, *Fort Myers News-Press* online readers began seeing video on the site in October 2006. "How we do video today is different from how we did video three months ago or six months ago or a year ago," says executive editor Kate Marymont. "So, it's constant evolution."[14]

That evolution took place as the *News-Press,* like other newspapers with competitive Web operations, found that the medium gives them an opportunity to do breaking news coverage instead of concentrating on just one edition per day.

So now, besides text and still photos, the Web's ability to deliver video relatively quickly has become a staple of that philosophy. "We want to be the first with video in this market," says Marymont. "TV is our primary competitor."[15]

The paper began equipping its reporters with small "point and shoot" cameras. They also received wireless-equipped laptops so they could file text and pictures from virtually anywhere. In effect, they became mobile journalists, or MoJos.

"We found that people respond so well to images that we started a program outfitting everyone on our staff, not just street people, not just reporters and photographers, but everyone: our copy editors, our managers, our page designers with the little point and shoots," says Marymont, "so that 140 people have a camera on their front seat. And it's paying off. We've had copy editors who are on their way to work got stuck in a traffic jam, so they sat there and they take pictures and they e-mail, you send it by their cell phone and we get it on our Web site."[16]

Almost as an afterthought, someone realized those little digital cameras were capable of shooting video as well as still pictures. So, in its evolution, the *News-Press* began adding video to the Web site in November 2006. "You're out there with your MoJo kit," says Cindy McCurry-Ross, the paper's senior managing editor, "and you can do across every platform. You can send in a text update, shoot photos, shoot quick video, and get it all on, especially on a breaking news situation."[17]

The video end of the coverage has gone through some growing pains. Many, but not all, of the reporters who have cameras have been thoroughly trained in using them to shoot video. Few know how to actually edit the video.

"I just gather some clips, do interviews on video," says the higher education beat writer Dave Breitenstein. He says he learned a lot of what to do by just playing with the point-and-shoot cameras, most of which are versions of the Nikon Coolpix. "I've learned to not just shoot something that's still. You know, make sure there's movement." And when he interviews a source, he just holds the camera up in front of the subject and uses it as he might an audio recorder for taping his notes. Once he's finished shooting, Breitenstein gives it to an editor in the online area to cut into a Web video story.[18]

MoJos on the Go

Many other newspapers are also adopting the MoJo model. "It is probably 60 percent of my time that is spent out," says mobile reporter Jeff Blackwell of the *Rochester Democrat & Chronicle.* One memorable assignment was the day New York governor Eliot Spitzer resigned. Blackwell took his video camera to a local diner to get reactions from patrons about the politician's downfall. "The picture and the sound show the expressions on their faces, the tone in their voices," says the reporter. "You could tell if they agreed with what he was doing or not."[19]

The newspaper industry magazine, *Editor & Publisher,* noted that the *Fort Myers News-Press* was ahead of the curve, but a number of other newspapers joined the trend to make reporters mobile and video-capable. The executive editor of the *Oregonian* in Portland, Peter Bhatia, said, "We are trying to equip more folks with media kits so that everything we could conceivably want, journalistically, can be gathered in the same setting."[20]

Indianapolis Star reporter Amy Bartner is one of those growing legions of MoJos, filing as many as five videos to the newspaper each week. She normally does not return to the newsroom to file the video. "I go into a Starbucks and transmit, or from a student union," says Bartner. "Anywhere I can find a quiet place to sit."[21]

One indication of how fast newspapers adopted video for their Web sites is that at the National Press Photographers Association TV News Workshop in 2008, newspaper still photographers outnumbered TV news photographers for the first time.[22]

One network newscast is setting a cross-platform milestone in videojournalism. *NBC Nightly News* has been running videos produced by the *New York Times* and the *Washington Post.*[23] On one such story, NBC anchorman Brian Williams's opening line was this: "Here now the reporting of *New York Times* reporter, Joe Berger, and Brent McDonald, whose voice you'll hear telling this story." The video had an MSNBC logo in the lower left corner and a *Times* logo in the lower right. It ran 2:23 on the NBC newscast, cut down from the five-minute story the *Times* had posted the day before on its Web site.[24]

The infinite paths on the Internet super highway also offer a variety of ways for newspapers and new media to collaborate to transmit their news video to the public. Yahoo is working with hundreds of newspapers in a consortium to boost traffic on news Web sites.[25]

How Newspaper and TV Video News Differ

Washingtonpost.com has become one of the standard bearers of the legions of newspapers turning to video storytelling. But that doesn't mean it has adopted the look of the typical TV news package or newscast. The *Post*'s style of video stories de-emphasizes the role of the reporter, has no time constraints, and can use a multimedia experience with links, graphics, and text to bring various elements of the story to life for the audience. "We can present in a sense a more pure emotional experience in the story simply because we can let the facts be conveyed by other essences of media that are draped around that video," says former managing editor/multimedia Tom Kennedy, who helped bring online video stories to prominence.[26]

That allows the videojournalists to concentrate on what the TV camera can do best, show people to people. The *Post's* videos aim to tell stories of peoples' experiences, through their eyes and let videojournalists work as still photographers traditionally have, observing, but not steering or shaping the drama of the story.

Instead of hiring videojournalists from TV, *washingtonpost.com* began training its own stable of VJs. One was Christina Pino-Marina, who started at the Web operation in 2000 as a reporter and writer. But it soon became clear to her that working in the new multimedia environment would require more than just writing.[27]

Her first attempt at video storytelling came when editors sent her to Florida to cover the presidential ballot counting. "Everything was on the fly," she recalls. Managers wanted her to file print stories, audio reports, and even dabble in this newfangled video storytelling tool.

Pino-Marina's first video report was working with another new VJ, Ben de la Cruz. "I wasn't really clear on the direction," she says. She got different feedback from different people; no one style seemed to fit all the *Post's* VJs. "And so, we were getting a little bit of everything and mixed signals from some of the editors. Some people wanted to see a reporter on camera, some people didn't and so it was a little bit of a free for all and an experimental phase." That experiment included finding out what video worked on the Web, what didn't, and making sure that the video stories stood out from the print product and didn't duplicate what was already in the paper.

Over the next few years, Pino-Marina did more video stories, usually working strictly as a reporter with other photographers. But in 2002 she picked up a camera to see what news videography was like. "So little by little, I tried doing some of those and seeing how it all worked together with the writing, because the assignment was primarily a writing assignment."

She liked the process and started getting some in-house training. When local military units were gearing up to go to Iraq, she focused on female soldiers and shot some of the video for the story. She got tips on holding the camera steady, maintaining her shots for at least ten seconds, getting a variety of shots such as wide, medium, and close-ups of soldiers tying their boots, "just little details like that," she says.

Later, Pino-Marina decided to try working alone on a story about a Georgetown sinkhole: "And I think I did make some early mistakes, moving the camera too much, zooming in and out, those types of things. But at the time things were so flexible here and they were so into people learning that it was just treated that way."

Before she left *washingtonpost.com* in 2008 to raise a family,[28] Pino-Marina felt that her transition from print reporter to VJ was complete. She described the video storytelling process as a way for things to come to life on-screen. "Voices, intonations, expressions, action, and emotion come through on camera in a way they sometimes can't in written stories."[29]

Newspaper Web Videojournalism Has Different Styles, Too

Documentary videojournalists who do stories measured in multiples of minutes instead of seconds are one of three types of solo videojournalism that *washingtonpost.com* displays on its Web site. Before the 2009 downsizing, the *Post*'s documentary VJs often had months to shoot and report, and hours of tape to wade through to produce their stories. Sometimes, however, the VJs were taken off their long-term assignments to do daily assignments on breaking news. The third category is using the *Post*'s print reporters to shoot video and sound bites for the Web site from stories they have been assigned for the newspaper.

With hundreds of reporters, that potentially puts considerable coverage on the street for *washingtonpost.com*. "If we can have a significant portion of them thinking video," says their trainer, Chet Rhodes, "every time they do a story, can this story be done in video as well, or is there a video component, or is there a visual component, in a way that newspaper reporters have never thought before, we are going to be fabulous. We are going to be so ahead of the game."

But for print reporters, taking on the added duty of producing video for their stories is voluntary. Those who do sign up receive training in very low-end camera gear, and in just the bare essentials in rudimentary videography. "Most of these people don't even know how to put a battery in a camera," says Rhodes. "It's not that they haven't done a lot of video, they haven't done a lot of technology." As a result, the neophyte videojournalists need to take baby steps, he says: "People don't even understand which side of the tape is up or down. So you really have to start with the very basics. You can't assume they know anything."

The gear is far from elaborate. When a newspaper correspondent comes in to check out equipment to go to an assignment, she will leave with a Panasonic Mini DV camera with a built-in microphone that fits in the palm of a hand. Also included is a small tripod, a box of mini DV tapes, a power cord, and battery charger. Everything together weighs about three pounds.

Once reporters turn in their tape, editors massage the video to put it on the Web.

"Right now the interest is very high," says Rhodes of the print reporters. "Actually getting them to do the video is actually hard. And the reason is, they know they're not good at it and they don't want to be embarrassed."

With such a large staff, it's understandable that some of the *Post*'s reporters take to the training better than others. "Motivation is driving this," says Rhodes. He says reporters who are not yet at the top of their game have the most to gain and see video assignments as a way to get ahead of their peers.

Indeed, intrepid print reporters who try solo videojournalism more than once do see improvement. "The first thing most people do is pretty bad," Rhodes says. "The second thing they do is a little better. The third thing they do is actually okay. And by the time they get to the fifth, sixth, seventh, eighth thing, if we can get them that far, we get stuff that's good."

Take Time to Do It Right

Newspaper Web editors have to determine whether a story merits the extra effort that video requires before producing a story. "Every day we make difficult choices: We cannot produce video with every article on the Web site," writes the *New York Times* video editor Ann Derry. "So we've chosen to provide our viewers with a sampling of the depth and breadth of *Times* journalism."[30]

But when newspaper VJs are set loose on a story, they usually don't have to worry about the multiple daily deadlines that their TV counterparts face. One major difference in the way the *washingtonpost.com* videojournalists approach stories from the way television news does its stories is the time that *Post* VJs have to devote to a mini-documentary. Ben de la Cruz has had repeated interviews that paid off in coaxing people out of their shell to reveal details about their lives. "You want to create an atmosphere where they're comfortable, where you're going to get actual moments and more honest answers and people will tell you things that they otherwise wouldn't," says the VJ. "You've got to spend time with people."[31]

On a series on veterans' post-traumatic stress, de la Cruz worked with a print reporter and interviewed one man three times. "It was only the third time, when I went back alone, when he gave me the real story in essence. And I was like 'Wow, it took three tries.' It took that much. But I can see why, this was a very touchy subject for people."

De la Cruz adds, "He was speaking vaguely the first few times, and I couldn't quite get it and . . . I would come back and try to edit the interview and would say it doesn't feel complete or not quite fitting for some reason."

Working as a solo videojournalist gave de la Cruz the flexibility to go back and give the vet's interview a third try. "He probably thought he was being very forthcoming initially, but he was most forthcoming in the end and it was very helpful," says the VJ. "It's not going to come out unless they trust you to some extent."

This is a simple box of gear that *washingtonpost.com* sends with its newspaper reporters for video assignments.

Washingtonpost.com's "Multimedia Cave" is equipped very much like editing rooms at TV stations.

Developing a Newspaper VJ Style

As a VJ, de la Cruz has developed his own style of storytelling. "I have people look right into the camera now instead of like looking at the interviewer," he says. Working for nine months on the Web site's "Being a Black Man," project, de la Cruz says he wanted his subjects to have more direct contact with viewers through the camera lens, looking directly at viewers instead of the traditional interview style of being focused on an interviewer alongside the camera. Those were personality-driven pieces and de la Cruz admits the style may not work for issue-oriented stories. Yet he continues to employ the device: "It's a subtly different way [to tell a story]. If you watch the video, you just notice you're kind of like in their face. So I think it kind of like automatically gives you a certain connection."

The emphasis for the newspaper Web VJs is to get away from traditional TV news storytelling. "We don't have standups," says de la Cruz. "We shoot in 16 by 9. We de-interlace our stuff so it's more film-like."

In fact, the *washingtonpost.com* Web site self-describes the journalists' work as "a new form of visual journalism" combining video and interactive media: "we are deliberately trying to create a new model of storytelling harkening back to what Marshall McLuhan once described as an 'acoustic space' that had more in common with cave paintings and oral storytelling tradition than the linear narrative forms that have flowed from text in the last 500 years."[32]

Click on the Web site's documentary link to discover the works of the *Post*'s VJs. It's a mixture of "slice of life" views and in-depth reporting captured by the journalists. Some, obviously, are better than others; some are more professional looking than others; some are more compelling to view than the rest.

But the stories labeled documentaries are not long by TV's thirty- or sixty-minute documentary standards. Ben de la Cruz did a natural sound story with no narration that runs 3:41 about a pastor comforting his Korean-American congregation after the Virginia Tech killings. The natural sound transmits the experience of what it was like in that particular group in the wake of the tragedy.

Christina Pino-Marina did another Virginia Tech follow up as well, a 2:29 story about how baseball brought the university community together. It starts focusing on kids handing out ribbons and interviewing a mother about why she wanted them involved in the event. Again, the story is told without narration, using only natural sound—including a 32-second moment of silence before a Hokies game—and sound bites with a lot of different shots from a variety of angles.

Washingtonpost.com also contains thinking-out-of-the-box storytelling examples, many of which could never be tried on broadcast news outlets. One is a series called "onBeing," which has different people talking in front of a studio backdrop, in a sequence of bites that are jump cuts. But people get to tell their own stories or to speak about whatever is on their minds.

Ben de la Cruz is one of the VJs who survived layoffs at *Washingtonpost.com*.

Another long-term, in-depth effort by Pino-Marina resulted in a comprehensive view of Cuba. Her video story on refugees was just one element in the multimedia page full of graphics and facts on the history of the U.S.-Cuba relationship and background on the embargo of the country.

A New Standard to Judge

So, overall, *washingtonpost.com*, along with other newspaper Web sites are breaking new ground in the realm of videojournalism. In 2007, the National Press Photographers Association issued awards for the first time in a category for online video and editing. Many of the judges had TV news videography backgrounds; their comments reflected their disdain for the upstart online videographers. "It is obvious," wrote Erica Simpson from San Diego's KGTV, "these were people who came mostly from newspapers and were trying to learn a craft. They were making basic mistakes in telling stories with pictures."[33]

Yet some of the TV judges admit they have a new challenge on their hands from the online videojournalists: "They have the advantage of a less-specific deadline and a longer format. It is the documentary style meeting the news kind of storytelling," wrote Mike Harrity of KUSA in Denver. "This kind of storytelling online will influence what we do on TV quite a bit."[34]

Nevertheless, over the breadth of the submitted work, online VJs have standards to live up to in the TV judges' eyes. "Since we have no bar set, since this is the first year NPPA has offered these categories," says Simpson, "we didn't want to set the bar too low and say this is what national award-winning online video looks like. We chose the best of the lot, but this is not where the bar of excellence should be."[35]

Despite those judges' comments and the downsizing at the *Post* and other newspaper Web sites, newspaper VJs are challenging television's status as the king of news video: their work is redefining what videojournalism is all about.

Discussion and VJ Exercise

1. What is the difference between a VJ and a MoJo? What are the similarities and differences in how they approach telling a story with video? How different are the cameras that VJs and MoJos use? What are the advantages or disadvantages of using either to shoot a video story?

2. Why do many newspapers choose not to emulate the TV news model of video storytelling for their Web sites? How are the models of a TV news package and a mini-documentary for a Web site different? Is one style better than the other? Why or why not?

3. How do viewers watch a TV news story? How do viewers on the Web watch a video news story? Can you report, shoot, write, and edit a story that is useful for viewers in both mediums, or are they so different that they require VJs to structure their stories differently for each?

4. Take the same story you wrote from the exercise in chapter 7 and now do it without the narration. Edit a seamless video essay with a beginning, middle, and end using nothing but your video, sound bites, and natural sound.

5. Have a colleague view both edited stories (narrated and non-narrated) and critique them. Which tells a better story? Which are you more adept and natural at creating? Are there skills you need to work on to improve one of the story types?

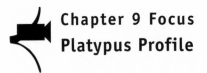

Chapter 9 Focus
Platypus Profile

Dirck Halstead already had a distinguished career working as *Time* magazine's White House photojournalist. Then, in the late 1990s he saw major changes coming. He became a videojournalist and has been working to convert other still news photographers ever since. "If you are working for the newspaper, you are going to be working for the Web," says Halstead. "What the Web wants is video . . . what the Web cares about is video."[1]

He founded Platypus, an organization dedicated to training photojournalists how to become videojournalists. "The fact is that when you start working in video, which means you are going from a spatial medium to a temporal medium, in which all these elements have to fit together, requires a tremendous amount of concentration and discipline," says Halstead.

"Watching people as they suddenly come awake, they're halfway through the course and watching the light bulbs go off, is a remarkable experience. They come in and they're catatonic and they go out involved. And another interesting thing that we've heard over and over again, that learning video and learning the disciplines actually make them much better still photographers."

The term Platypus is based on the unusual Australian mammal that lives both in the water and on land. It seemed an apt name for the new organization, muses Halstead, because "this creature was a total weird thing . . . and it had survived because of its adaptability."

One of the early Platypus converts was Roger M. Richards. He also worked at the White House as a photographer for the *Washington Times*. "I tiptoed into it," says Richards, who worked as a videojournalist for the *Norfolk Virginian-Pilot* from 2001 until 2007 and is now an independent filmmaker and photographer.[2] "It was a funny time," he adds. "Other photographers looked at us as threats. They saw us as heretics."[3]

Richards, like other still photographers saw the career-changing trend and decided to get on board early. "You're either going to adapt or you're going to go extinct."

What Platypus specializes in is teaching photographers how to work as solo videojournalists, ones who can produce the mini-documentary style of storytelling without narration. "What you see in those videos are inherently much better than what you see on television," says Halstead. "Why? Because they're being produced by creative individuals who are professionals who have worked in photography all of their lives. They understand light. They understand composition. And so, once you teach them how to sequence and once you teach them how to edit, the quality of the work they produce is much better than what a crew will produce."

Richards has been on the Platypus faculty since 2005. "There's a way we teach it. There's a respect for the story and the subject," he says. Besides teaching the non-narration documentary style of video storytelling, Platypus also emphasizes trying to achieve a one-on-one intimacy with interviewees. Some people just like to unload their troubles on an empathetic listener Richards says, "You're like a confessor. They feel they have somebody to listen to them."

The technique of listening without interrupting or talking is hard for some classically trained reporters who take the Platypus course. Yet the instructors say the converts are excited to learn the new way of storytelling that is far different from the traditional TV method of reporter-narrated stories.[4]

Chapter 10

They've Got MoJo, Baby—
How VJs Put It All Together

There is no single way to approach shooting, writing, and editing a story as a solo videojournalist, yet there are similarities in the way VJs operate as well. This chapter profiles VJs from TV, a newspaper, and an independent news website to show how various VJs go solo.

Jerry Barlar—WKRN, Nashville

Jerry Barlar is standing outside a barbershop on a bright, blue-sky afternoon in Lewisburg, an hour south of Nashville.[1] His VJ piece that spring day is to get the community's reaction as they bury a local marine who was killed in Iraq.

Jerry spent nearly fifteen years as a WKRN-News 2 videographer, then worked on the News 2 assignment desk. Well versed already in shooting and editing, Jerry admits his biggest challenge when he converted to a VJ at the ABC affiliate was tackling the writing. He says the work is more taxing, yet his writing is "coming along," and he says that by working on the project from beginning to end by himself, "You're a little more prideful at the end of the day."

Originally assigned a beat as the outdoors VJ, Jerry has since branched out to do general assignment stories as well. Another point about his new position is not lost on this father of two, who now even does live shots from in *front* of the camera: "I'll do anything that makes me more valuable," he says.

For this story Jerry is wearing a tie, burgundy shirt, and dress slacks instead of his normal blue jeans and open-collared shirt. He also brought a jacket to

Jerry Barlar shoots cover video after interviewing his subject.

wear for his live shot that afternoon. Barlar won the right to do this day's top story by going "off beat" and winning praise for an earlier story he did about the fallen marine.

A few days before, he'd been assigned to cover the family of the deceased marine, who were willing to talk to the local media. Jerry told them he wanted to do a story about the soldier's life, not his death. He put the story to music, using just family members' comments without any narration. "It was a physically and emotionally draining story," he says, trying to get all his interviews after 2:00 p.m. and getting stories ready for both the 5:00 and 6:00 o'clock newscasts. But he ranked it as one of his best since he started as a VJ a year and a half earlier.

In that morning's news meeting in the station's combination newsroom/studio, Jerry's expertise about the town and the subject helps cement the day's work plan. "This is the third soldier they've lost in Iraq," he tells those assembled for the meeting.

The news director decided to put extra resources into the story to make sure it is well covered. "What I see emerging is the story of a small town that's paid an enormous price," Steve Sabato tells everyone as he sips from his bottle of Perrier. His idea is to "swarm" the town to do "poignant VJ pieces." "I'd like two powerful VJ pieces focused around individuals." Besides Barlar, he sends another VJ to pursue a different angle and a satellite truck with a two-person crew to handle the main coverage for the 5:00 and 6:00 live shots. "Now we can lead a couple of shows with it," Sabato finishes.[2]

A story focused around an individual is just what Jerry comes up with. He befriends a barber, whose brother had gone to school with the marine. He shot video inside and did an interview as well; now Jerry is outside getting cover video for the story. "This is a tough story to do as a VJ," he remarks. The funeral is at 2:00; his package with a live shot is scheduled to air at 4:00.

But one advantage he has working alone is the rapport he can establish with a subject. When he first meets someone he might like to interview, "I just put my camera down to put people at ease. I try to get to know the person and their personality," before shooting the interview. He says the situation is often more relaxed than with a two-person crew and, as a result, people open up more. "It puts people more at ease and I think you'll get more candid answers." That may be because as a husky, six-plus-footer, Jerry has the skills and confidence to hand-hold the video camera. He says he shoots without a tripod 90 percent of the time.

Doing live reports on newscasts was something Jerry Barlar,
who converted to a VJ from a photographer, had to learn on the job.

VJ guru Michael Rosenblum trained Jerry and other WKRN solo videojournalists, but unlike the Rosenblum story model, which dictates that VJ stories should be focused on just one person, "There's no cookie cutter approach," Jerry says, "I can tell both sides of a story.

"I start writing the story in my head. Anything I need to know, I try to get it on tape."

The station's satellite truck is a few blocks away. The VJ drives there and ingests the video into his nonlinear editor while listening to interviews and taking notes from that. Once he finishes his script, Jerry calls it into the station for approval then attacks the editing. Then, with plenty of time to spare, he strolls in front of the camera set up for the 4:00 p.m. live shot and delivers his intro and tag to his package flawlessly.

With all the new tasks the VJ has taken on, the writing is still the toughest part admits the former videographer, "My work has improved a ton in the year and a half I've been doing it, but in five years I hope to report and write as well [as the reporters]."

Angela Grant—InstantNewsWestU.com, Houston

The sign leaning against the stroller blares, "My mommy's faster than your mommy!"[3]

Angela Grant is on her knees getting a wide shot of the sign and the stroller with its beaming occupant. She moves in to get a close-up of the sign, then walks a few steps and shoots a couple of more angles. Those shots accomplished, she slings her camera strap over her shoulder and walks down University Boulevard to continue gathering video to tell a story about this community's part in the Chevron Houston Marathon.

Her business card for InstantNewsWestU.com lists Angela as a mobile journalist, but she prefers the term multimedia reporter. "The reporter is the one that's talking to people, going out, learning the facts, examining documents, and finding out what the story is and telling people the story," she says. "That's exactly what I do; I just have a choice about what tool I want to use to tell the story."

A 2006 multimedia journalism graduate of the University of Texas, Angela can write a story with text, do a photo slide show with audio, make interactive graphics, and shoot and edit video. She has done it all for her hyperlocal Web news organization that covers the West University Place and Bellaire communities of Houston. Covering the government beats in the two enclave cities often requires just plain old shoe leather reporting instead of the technical skills, however. "Most stuff government is doing is boring video. It's just more efficient to write it out," she says.

But on this cool morning in mid-January, dressed in a leather jacket and blue jeans, Grant has her Sony HDV camera in hand and a fanny pack with a

Sometimes Angela Grant asks interview subjects what they had
for breakfast to put them at ease and to check her audio levels.

wireless microphone and batteries. She is putting her multimedia skills to work
as a solo videojournalist for the annual marathon that cuts through the heart
of West U, as the city is called.

With all the action, sound, and people, it's a story tailor-made for video. Her
aim is to do a two-minute piece with bites and natural sound, but no reporter
narration. "The first thing you'd think of is shooting runners," says Angela. The
major Houston media cover the winners and the grand scale of the event. "But
that's not the whole story," says the hyperlocal reporter, "and in fact, that is not
the focus of my story. The focus of my story is the people that live there, resi-
dents and their reaction, you know, what's their role in the marathon. And so I
was really looking around for people, for people that were really into it. People
holding funny signs, you know, cheering, yelling, stuff like that."

Well before the runners arrive, Angela stakes out a two-block section near
the thirteen-mile marker, the halfway point in the marathon near the West U
City Hall on University Boulevard. The first person she seeks for an interview
is the mayor. But he is out of town; instead, she grabs the mayor pro-tem,
hooks a wireless microphone to his lapel, and asks him to hold the transmit-

ter. "I'm going to ask you some throw away questions to set my audio levels," she tells him. "Okay," he responds. "What are you having for breakfast?" she adds.

Angela doesn't even carry a tripod with her for this event. For the hand-held interview, she runs her right hand through the strap on the side of the lightweight camera, holds her left hand underneath, and lowers her elbows to steady the camera.

Once she finishes that interview, she patrols the boulevard, keeping her eyes open for good opportunities for interviews, video, and natural sound. As the lead runners make their way past city hall, an oldies band strikes up a song. Angela grabs a sequence of the band, the runners, and a reaction shot of a couple dancing to the tune. Then she moves up University, grabbing a variety of shots along the way.

"Look at that!" she exclaims. The VJ has spotted a runner approaching dressed in a Statue of Liberty outfit. Angela quickly unslings her camera and gets a shot of him coming toward her, then jogs alongside a few steps as well.

Just ahead is where she wants to be, a station where volunteers are handing out water in paper cups to the runners. Angela spends several minutes getting shots, some with a strong foreground of cups lined up, others of people in colorful costumes holding cups for the runners.

At one spot she asks one woman for an interview. The woman declines, however, saying she doesn't want to appear on camera, but would talk for a text article.

A few minutes later she finds a more agreeable subject. This woman asks who the interview is for. "It's a little video for our website," Angela responds; "I write for them." She rolls the camera while asking the woman her name and asks her to spell it before asking questions about why she is at the event.

The hunt for good video continues. At one point, Angela lies flat on her belly to get a low-angle shot of discarded paper cups with runners passing in the background.

In her multimedia training at the University of Texas, Angela learned HTML, Flash, how to create a blog, how to write a good text story, and how to edit audio and video. But she did not learn how to shoot video. She says that is something she wishes had been in the curriculum.

Instead, she picked up the art of videography at her first job out of school at the *San Antonio Express-News.* "I was the first with the title 'multimedia anything,'" she says. She did an average of four video stories a week in her three years at the *Express-News,* constantly learning about what makes a good video story. She admits her shooting and video storytelling skills improved immensely after the newspaper brought in a TV news videographer and some documentary filmmakers for two workshops for the multimedia staff.

Now this multimedia reporter is so immersed in videojournalism that she even created a Web site, newsvideographer.com, on which she blogs about the art and hosts discussions and links to other VJ sites.

Working her way back toward city hall, Angela spots a spectator holding a tall glass with a mimosa. The woman agrees to an interview, holding the glass in her right hand and the mic transmitter in the other. During the conversation, Angela learns that the woman is celebrating her birthday and is happy that all these people have joined her party.

After the interview, the woman points out some kids with an unusual sign. "Why don't you do what you were doing before I came and I'll get a few shots of you," Angela tells the kids. While shooting, the youngsters shout exhortations, repeating the sign's message, promising they'll do their homework if the runners go faster.

A few steps ahead she grabs a natural sound sequence of a family greeting a runner who high-fives everyone and then continues on his twenty-six-mile journey. Across the street people are handing out fruit to marathoners and Angela grabs shots of that as well.

It's 9:15 a.m. The multimedia reporter has been on the scene since 7:00 and has thirty minutes of video. "I have enough. I'm going back to the office to edit." She loads her gear back into the bright red compact panel van with logos proclaiming "Constantly Updated Neighborhood News," the organization's Web address, and a tip line for story ideas.

Angela normally works a five-day week, trying to post at least three stories a day for each of the Web sites covering West U and Bellaire. That often requires twelve- to fifteen-hour days to gather all the information and prepare six stories for the two sites. She had not tried to access her office, a few blocks from the race route, before on a Sunday, however, and discovers she can't get access to the tenth floor from the locked elevators. So, she drives a few miles to a Starbucks where she can have coffee, plug in her laptop to edit, plus feed the video and text to the InstantNewsWestU.com Web site through a Wi-Fi connection.

She has chosen to do the story without writing anything to narrate. "The only time I actually narrate stuff with my voice is if it's a complicated story that I believe people need either background information or kind of technical information that I need to better explain it so that they can understand. Other than that, I hardly ever will narrate a story with my voice."

At 10:15 she begins capturing the video into her MacBook with Final Cut Express, a cheaper version of Final Cut Pro. "I don't log. I find it is faster if I capture the b-roll in one-minute chunks." She also captures all of her interviews. "For interviews, I capture the whole interview and choose what I want," she says. "I used to be diligent about logging . . . but I find it faster this way."

Thirty minutes later, after capturing all the video, Angela organizes her story by putting in sound bites first. "I'm going to pull down my interview clips first so I have an idea of timing. I started out with the mayor pro-tem, his comments, because he kind of provided . . . an overall view," says Angela, saying she wants to structure the story with a beginning, middle, and end. "And I really like the lady at the end, 'It's my birthday and this is a huge party.' And so I thought that was a really good ending."

She finishes laying the sound bites on the timeline at 10:59. There is about one minute of interviews. Now she begins to put in the natural sound that will provide moments for the audience to experience what it was like to witness the marathon in West U.

As she tweaks the story, she begins with natural sound up full with the video. "I knew from being there, there were several, several clips that were the absolute best natural sound. And that's why I started with the girls who were like, 'Run faster and I'll do my homework,'" says Angela, mimicking the girls in falsetto. "And that's just funny."

She structures her timeline with four audio channels and two video channels, using V1, A1, and A2 for sound bites and V2, A3, and A4 for natural sound. "When people see a video story, they're experiencing that very like in real life. And that sound is part of that experience. So I want to be able to mix the a-roll audio with the b-roll audio, so you have to have it on separate tracks."

"I like to do the b-roll in one-minute chunks, because you can look at it quickly." She goes through and renames the captured b-roll chunks from numbers to descriptions that help her find what she needs to lay it on the timeline quickly when she wants it.

When working on the sequence of the man who paused for his family's greeting, Angela says, "I want to get that to match up more." She stretches the shot and natural sound back toward the beginning so that a wide shot of the man matches to a medium shot of him raising his hands. The sequence ends with him turning around and continuing the race.

"I think I'm done with the b-roll," she says at 11:35. "I'm just going through and clean up the audio levels a little bit." She puts key frames, which she calls dots, at points on the audio timeline where she wants to raise or lower the sound. Then she drags the dots up or down to change the audio levels. The final audio touch is putting dissolves on the natural sound tracks to make the transitions smoother. "I will also do it on the others [the sound bites] if it sounds abrupt," she says.

There are still several more steps to complete the project before posting it on the Web site. First is putting in supers to identify the people interviewed. There is no standard style for the company; Angela uses a style she created herself. "I use drop shadow at least so that it stands out from the background." She also creates a super with her byline and e-mail that goes over black at the end of the story.

With that closing super over black, the story runs 1:50, just shy of her two-minute target.

The next step is to make sure that the story has progressive instead of alternating scan lines. She selects an option in the software for that. "You have to deinterlace it for the Web," says Angela, "otherwise it looks terrible."

She renders the project and processes it into a QuickTime file. She exports the file in an NTSC 720 X 480, 16:9 format. Even though she shot in high definition, she does not process it or load it to the Web that way. She says the small increase in quality is not worth the time it takes to do the extra processing. As it is, the standard definition processing takes about twenty minutes.

While the computer is chugging along working on the video, Angela uses WordPress to start loading the video and text set-up for InstantNewsWestU.com. She writes a headline, "Marathon Runners Find Festive Route Through West U." and a short description of the video. She also decides to load it all on the company's companion site, InstantNewsBellaire.com, but revises the description, moving the West University Place reference from the beginning of the sentence to the end.

It's 12:22. "We'll be out of here in no time," says the multimedia reporter. All her work on the Web has been in draft mode so far. She hits "Publish" and her hyperlocal video story goes out to the Web for the whole world to see.[4]

Dan Weaver—KUSA, Denver

KUSA-TV has long been known as a "photographers' shop," a destination for news videographers who want to hone their skills and craft in a station and market that appreciate good photography.[5] One backpack journalist came to KUSA thinking he would be able to do just that rather than tack on the task of reporting. Before arriving in Denver, Dan Weaver worked ten- to eleven-hour days, five days a week as a one-man band at the Gannett TV station, WLTX, in Columbia, South Carolina. He got burnt out on the experience: "I think coming in every day and doing that much work and having that much pressure on you and going out by yourself every day, it, it takes a toll. It's tough," says Weaver.

Originally a music major on a scholarship at the University of South Carolina, Dan switched majors after his second journalism class. Although he can do both reporting and videography, he prefers being a photographer only. "I like working with reporters; I think generally two heads are better than one. I can learn and feed off of whomever I'm working with and hopefully they can do the same with me. I think the end result is a better story."

So, even though KUSA hired him as a photographer in 2004, his reputation as a one-man band preceded him; Weaver was soon working a few days a week at KUSA as a backpack journalist. "I'm happy doing what I'm doing now. One day a week I think is fine for me," he says. "But I at least have a couple of days a week where I don't have to worry about that, that I can just go out and shoot vo/sots or work with a reporter."

One of those BPJ days is Sunday, usually a slow news day filled with features. Yet on this Sunday in August, the desk has assigned him to both a VJ story and a reporter's exclusive story that will need two videographers.

Coming into the morning news meeting, Dan had received an e-mail tip about a local charitable group sponsoring a free clothing spree for the Denver Children's Home. "Are you interested in this kids clothing giveaway?" he asks the producer. He gets an affirmative reply. But Dan says it may only be a vo/sot instead of a package since he will have to be at the Denver jail for the other story an hour later.

He prefers working as a photographer, so when Dan Weaver works as a VJ he carries a larger camera than most who work solo.

The first story is at a department store in Lakewood, a twenty-five-minute drive from the station. Since he's on a tight schedule, Dan parks his vehicle and hustles into the store where the kids' shopping spree is just getting underway. He carries his Sony DVCAM with an Anton Bauer Ultralight mounted on top, a medium-weight Gitzo tripod and wireless mic.

He mics up his first interviewee with a view looking down one clothing aisle. He walks to the right side of the camera, the side away from the viewfinder, and asks a few questions there. But he notices the interviewee shifting, so as he asks another question, Dan walks back to check the viewfinder, adjusts the framing and then moves back to the camera's right side again as the interviewee begins to respond.

For the next interview, after changing angles and hooking up the microphone, he stays on the left side of the camera to get the subject looking a different direction from the first interviewee.

With no time to lose, the organizers hook him up with thirteen-year-old Geavanni to follow as she shops. He straps the wireless mic to her, saying, "You go ahead and do your shopping. Ignore me and go right ahead." The girl and her counselor from the home, wearing a Kid Spree t-shirt, head off through the forest of aisles. Dan follows with the camera and tripod balanced on his shoulder.

Keeping his eye on the camera's eyepiece instead of the viewfinder, Dan gets several shots of the girl shopping and talking with the counselor. He normally uses the tripod, usually with three legs open, but since space is tight here, Dan folds them together to use it like a monopod. Then while the girl is in a changing room, he does an impromptu interview with the counselor, pulling the shotgun mic off the tripod-mounted camera and holding it out with his left hand to conduct the interview.

But the wireless mic is his main sound source. He uses it to get natural sound from the girl as she skitters from aisle to aisle, rack to rack, checking prices and sizes. "What you got the calculator for? How much money you got?" Dan asks.

"$125," she replies.

He removes the DVCAM from the tripod and follows Geavanni into the fabric jungle, bracing himself against racks and pillars to get the steadiest shots possible. "I try to keep it on the tripod as much as possible," he says. "But I was having trouble getting some of the tight shots I needed for editing." He shoots up at some hanging clothes, then tilts down to the girl and her helper. He tucks the camera under his right arm and shoots a few shots from that angle when calamity strikes.

The bracket holding the wireless microphone receiver on the rear of the camera breaks and is dangling from the cables attaching it to the camera's mic inputs. As it swings, the camera also sways and makes any video unsteady and unusable. Fortunately Dan is prepared. He takes two heavy rubber bands from around his shotgun microphone and uses them to strap the wireless mic bracket back onto the camera.

As he returns to shooting the b-roll, Geavanni's counselor asks whether Dan has any more work to do that day. "I've actually had to leave five minutes ago for the Denver County Jail," Dan replies.

But before he leaves, he gets one last shot, one that might work for the closing of a package. "Did you have fun?" he asks the girl. "You ready for school?" Geavanni answers, "I love school," as she weaves her way through another clothing aisle, walking away from the camera.

Shooting the Kid Spree took only thirty minutes, but packing up at 10:40, Dan is under pressure to get to the county jail by 11:00. Driving to the jail he has to make a phone call to check on one fact, however. He carried no notebook into the assignment, never wrote a word. He says he always asks people to spell their name on camera and keeps notes in his head. But this time he forgot to ask how to spell the thirteen-year-old girl's name. When he reaches one of the event's organizers from his cell phone, he jots down the girl's name on a dashboard notepad. "Thank you, Shannon. I appreciate it," he tells the organizer.

That's one of the disadvantages of working solo, he laments. "When I have time, it wouldn't be a problem," but this time getting the girl's name just slipped through the cracks because of the rush to get to the next assignment.

He also wonders whether he has enough video to turn the story into a package, or whether it will just be a vo/sot. He thinks he does not have enough video and sound to do his preferred method of doing a story, using only natural sound and bites without any narration. "Since it's tight on sound, I would guess I might voice it," Dan muses. "I've got a bunch of stuff with her."

Dan has close-cropped brown hair, a stud protruding from his left ear, a movie idol face, and baritone voice—a combination that TV viewers might find appealing. But when asked if he ever considered becoming a full-time reporter in front of the camera instead of being behind the camera, Dan merely says, "I like shooting too much," and repeats that he applied to KUSA to be a photographer.

He dresses the part, too. Instead of tie, slacks, and a jacket, Dan comes to work this day in a lime green pullover shirt, faded blue jeans, and comfortable walking shoes. "I like working Sundays," he says. "It's relaxed."

Dan rolls into the Denver County Jail parking lot at 11:14 for his next assignment, this one strictly as a videographer. He meets another photographer, Ken Mostek, and they wait for reporter/anchor Cheryl Preheim. Once the team is assembled, they go through a security check and set up in an interview room. Ken will be operating the primary camera for an interview with an inmate who recently pleaded guilty to drunk driving and killing a mother and her two children on a Denver street. Dan will operate the camera shooting cutaways and the reporter's questions. The inmate cries during most of the interview and apologizes to the family and says if anyone ever wants to drink and drive, he hopes they will think first about this interview and how he has ruined not only the victims' lives, but his family's as well.

As they are talking, Dan shoots wide shots and close-ups of the convict's hands and then moves the camera a bit closer in the tight quarters for a better shot of the reporter. When Cheryl finishes her questions, she turns to the two videojournalists and asks if they have any questions; neither cameraman has any.

The jailhouse interview finished, Dan packs up his gear, then stops for a sandwich and brings it back to the station. Dan tells the producer, Preston Benson, that he has enough video to turn the kids clothing story into a minute package instead of a vo/sot. Benson gives him the go ahead, "All right, cool. You got it."

Yet he does not have an infinite amount of time to organize his material. It's the typically tight schedule for a VJ. But one advantage he has is already being aware of each shot he has on tape. "I usually don't have to go back and log my video," he says. "I know what's there." He says he'll take whatever time he has before the deadline to complete the edited story. "If I get four hours, it'll take me four hours. If I have an hour and a half, it'll take me an hour and a half."

One afternoon the station sent him out solo into the mountains to cover a soldier's funeral. He wrote the story in the car on the way back to the city, choosing the bites as best he could remember them. When he got to the station he put the script in the computer, edited the story, and had the lead on the five o'clock newscast.

In one of the station's edit bays, Dan is putting his bites on the nonlinear editor's timeline to organize the shopping spree story. Then he turns to a computer in the edit bay and types the script into the newsroom system. It's now 3:05 and he groans as he writes. "I'd much prefer a nat/package than . . ." his voice trails off leaving the thought unfinished. "It certainly isn't something special. Let's see what Preston has to say."

In the newsroom, Dan tells the producer, "It's nothing special. It is what it is." But Benson approves the script and Dan returns to the edit bay.

In the middle of editing the clothing story, he's called out to search for a two shot needed for the inmate story, which is the newscast's lead. He finds that and goes back to his booth to wrap up his own editing. He manipulates each piece of audio as he inserts it to get the sound just right. When it's finished, the story runs 1:18. He puts in audio dissolves and uploads the edited package to the server. He turns to the newsroom computer system again to write his supers for bites in the script as well so they can be inserted when the package airs live.

The backpack journalist has one more reporting task. It takes Dan fifteen minutes to write a story on the clothing spree for the KUSA Web site. He finishes in plenty of time to watch his story air at 5:38.

Christine Lee—From Newspaper to TV

Christine Lee pulls her car into a parking lot at a workout club in Fort Myers, Florida.[6] It's early January and after exhausting other efforts to find more newsworthy stories, the solo videojournalist's back-up plan for the day is to do a feature on how well people are keeping their New Year's resolutions to hit the gym and get in shape.

She's not on assignment for one of the market's TV stations, however. Christine is a VJ for the *News-Press*, the local newspaper. She's been working at the job a little over a year. Instead of a newspaper career though, Christine aspires to be a TV reporter. In some ways, this story at the fitness center is helping her get in shape for the career she has been working toward since she was fifteen years old.

A Southern California native, Christine says she has been "doing broadcast journalism" since she was a student at Beverly Hills High School. In college, she did several internships including stints at CNN and a local Korean language cable channel. She even went to South Korea to shoot a documentary for one of her classes at UCLA.

Fresh out of college with a degree from the prestigious film school, Christine went knocking on news directors' doors looking to get that first break in TV news. Despite her skills at both reporting and videography, and after several months of searching, the news directors never called with a job offer.

Then Christine met a Gannett corporate recruiter at a convention of the Asian American Journalists Association. To get her start in television news would have meant beginning in markets much smaller than Fort Myers and with a considerably smaller paycheck as well. So Christine jumped at the chance to become a Web VJ at the Gannett-owned *News-Press*. "This opportunity just kind of happened to fall at the right place at the right time," she says. "And it happened to be tailored exactly toward what I was interested in, which is reporting on camera."

It's the kind of job opportunity that aspiring videojournalists did not have a few years ago. "This opportunity gave me the chance, the creativity to explore different types of storytelling, not having to deal so much with time restraints, how long my pieces could be, what the subject could be about," says Christine. "So, it has given me the learning opportunity to just try things out on my own and not many people get that opportunity right out of college."

Inside the fitness facility, the newspaper VJ uses many of the techniques that are common to TV videographers. When she interviews a man working out on one machine, she "dresses" the lavaliere mic cable through his shirt and around his back so it's not visible on camera.

Later, she approaches a woman sitting on a weight bench for an interview, "I try to hide my camera whenever I can when I first approach somebody, because I want them to see me as a person asking them a question rather than seeing a big machine coming towards them."

Even though she would rather work strictly as a reporter with another photographer, the VJ does see advantages to working alone: "If you're by yourself," she says, "number one, it's one person versus two so it's a little bit less intimidating and the fact that you have a smaller camera . . . might also help, too." Yet she admits a reporter in a two-person crew could ask her photographer to stay in the background while she tries to establish rapport with an interviewee as well.

Though she does some things that viewers would see in typical TV news packages, some of her techniques are different. Her *News-Press* video packages often open with a standup, something TV reporters rarely do.

True, TV reporters do begin their *live* reports on camera before rolling their recorded packages. That is an experience that Christine misses and longs for in the Web world. "I want to be able to have that feeling of urgency, that butterfly you get in your stomach, you know, when you know you're going to be live."

To help her get to that point, Christine received critiques of her work from mentors in TV news. The *News-Press,* owned by the Gannett Corporation, also let her consult with the news staff from some Gannett-owned TV stations.

Unlike the newspaper's MoJos, Christine's job title is different: video reporter. She doesn't write stories for the Web, she doesn't do short videos of breaking news events as the MoJos do; instead she focuses on doing what those in TV news call a package: a video story she reports and narrates.

Christine carries a full set of video gear. That includes a Sony HDV mini-DV camera capable of shooting in high definition, a tripod, microphones, and lights. The more professional gear just reinforces Christine's resolve to avoid YouTubish video. "I want to be a storyteller. I'm going to be a storyteller. I'm not going to put up raw clips."

Yet unlike larger newspapers that have a following for their mini-documentary and narrated video stories, the *News-Press* just could not muster much of an audience for its VJ stories. "If we can't get people to watch two and a half minutes of a pretty good story that Christine does, we're certainly not going to get them to come back for a serialized installment type of documentary," says managing editor Mackenzie Warren. As a result, unlike larger newspaper Web sites, which do have a national and international audience for in-depth videos, the online video news audience for the *Fort Myers News-Press* seems content with local, smaller, less investigative video stories.

Christine Lee's VJ work took her from a newspaper Web site to a job in TV news.

"The hard news beats out the soft news all the time," Warren says.

That audience preference brought the evolution of video at the *News-Press* full circle. The genre of narrated VJ stories came to an end sixteen months after it started when Lee resigned to take a position at a television station in Arizona.

When she left the *News-Press,* Christine landed a job at KNAZ, a Gannett-owned TV station in Flagstaff, Arizona. Just like many others in the Gannett chain, Christine started her *television* career as a backpack journalist, very similar to the work she performed at the *News-Press* as a solo videojournalist.

"The pressure is on, that's for sure," she wrote of her new job, "but I'm grateful for the opportunity. It seems that my regular task involves shooting and editing a report (or two), writing a print version of it to accompany my video report online."[7]

At the new job, Christine used the same type of cameras she used in Fort Myers, but unlike that job, Christine also was called on to do live shots to introduce her video packages. "The live shots are fun—sometimes I do it by a chromakey inside the studio, and sometimes I go outside and I don't get a teleprompter . . . in both scenarios, it just happens . . . I thought I'd be more nervous, but it's actually not as bad as I feared . . ."[8]

Yet after working at KNAZ only a few months, the station closed its news operation. Another Gannett station in Phoenix, KPNX hired Christine as a multimedia journalist. Now she covers traffic in the morning and does stories for the afternoon newscasts as a multimedia reporter and VJ.[9] After three stops, all working as a solo videojournalist Christine says, "I'm getting faster at putting things together—shooting, especially logging and writing." As a result, her Phoenix editors had so much confidence in her abilities, they sent her to the Winter Olympics in Vancouver as part of the group of Gannett stations covering the event.[10]

Discussion and VJ Exercise

1. What are the similarities and differences in the VJs styles? Does the medium VJs work for dictate the style of video story they produce? Are VJs working in TV allowed to produce natural sound stories? Can VJs working on Web outlets narrate their stories?
2. Some of the VJs profiled say they would prefer to work in a two-person team to shoot their stories? Why? What changes would make it easier, more efficient, or practical for one person to do solo videojournalism?
3. Given the changes in the media over the last several years, is it practical for a VJ to think about moving to a position in a two-person video storytelling crew later in their career? What kind of career do you have mapped out? Is being a VJ your ultimate goal? How can being a VJ be a stepping-stone to something you would like to pursue later in your career?
4. Do you think it is easier to convert to being a VJ if one starts out as a reporter or a photographer? Why?
5. How can a VJ continue to grow and develop skills if he or she would like to maintain a career as a VJ? Are there organizations where one can get extra training to continue to make them valuable to their news organization or as a freelancer?

Chapter 10 Focus
Work Smarter by Saving Time

Time-management tips have been interspersed throughout this book as they relate to each task the VJ has to accomplish at various points in doing a story. Time management is so crucial to meeting deadlines that successful VJs have to make the most of every minute.

In Denver, KUSA-TV backpack journalist Kevin Torres "backtimes" his tasks each day to make sure he gets his stories in on time. "When I go over on time with one thing I cut from another," he says.[1]

Since VJs must do the work of a typical two-person crew, a comprehensive list of time-management tips from the beginning to the end of the story process can help solo videojournalists meet their deadlines.

Time Management Tips for the Solo Videojournalist

- Check out your equipment before the assignment. The scene of a news story is not the time to find out that a crucial piece of gear is not working. Fixing it before you leave could save you time in driving back to the office or another location to get the equipment fixed.
- Carry a small tool kit to repair items in the field. At the minimum carry a screwdriver, pliers, gaffers tape, and rubber bands. Also carry spares of essential items such as batteries and tape or other recording media.
- Get comfortable with your gear. Time spent fussing with equipment you are unfamiliar with could be better spent on actually reporting and shooting the story. Master your gear and shoot it right the first time so that you don't waste time having to repeat any shots.
- Set your shot and then roll to record it. Recording while zooming and establishing a shot just wastes time later in ingesting and finding editable shots.
- It may save time to establish rapport with a subject first without using the camera. Then once rapport is established, the shooting and on-camera interviews may go more smoothly and quickly.
- Although collaboration is often good, it can also be a hindrance. Solo videojournalists do not have to rely on communicating with a photographer to get what they want; they know when to roll the camera and are intimately familiar with their footage after shooting b-roll and interviews. That may save time by writing the story from the knowledge of the shots and interviews that are in your head instead of logging the video.
- If there is time, log your video, especially the bites and natural sound. That can save time later by ingesting only the video you need to edit the story.

- If time is of the essence, VJs may not be noticed and could be less likely to be stopped by curious onlookers. Don't call attention to yourself if your goal is to get in and get out quickly. Use the small camera and ability to get in and out of a scene with less intrusion to your advantage. If time is not of the essence, take time to chat with folks. It might pay off with useful information for that story you are working on or in a worthy story idea later.
- VJs working alone have more control of their schedule than a two-person crew. Keep an eye on the clock so that time doesn't slip away when working on a deadline. Don't procrastinate in setting up interviews or shooting; make time work for you; set interim deadlines to give yourself time to log crucial video, write the story, edit, and get feedback from others before the story airs.
- Since their hands are tied up with shooting a story, VJs need to find a system to remember names and facts for their stories: the camera may be their notebook or a small notepad may be required to jot down notes and ideas between shots. Jotting down names and facts on paper can save time later instead of trying to find the information by searching through the video for it.
- If a phrase or way to express the story hits you while you see the shot in the viewfinder, write it down. That may be the idea that sells the story and you'll kick yourself if you can't remember it later.
- If equipped properly for researching, writing, and editing, a VJ can save commuting time by working from home.
- Use the time you save by working alone to polish your work: do more than one draft of the script; show the edited piece to someone to get feedback before airing or publishing it.

Chapter 11

Think Ahead to Beat the Competition
and Be Ready for the Future

The retrenchment of the mainstream media may mean we will never again see the likes of Walter Cronkite, Tom Brokaw, or Peter Jennings, who became household names as they delivered the day's news in our living rooms.[1] Yet the efficiency of working alone, the increasing use of VJs and the unprecedented explosion of new media video opportunities give solo videojournalists an opportunity to make their mark and establish their own brand in a niched market for video storytelling.

The downsizing of the established media means fewer journalists will have the largesse of major companies to back them in the pursuit of their stories. So those who seek to brand themselves as twenty-first-century VJs will have to not only improve their writing and video skills, they will have to nurture their enterprising skills: digging out untold stories, developing them in creative ways, and then finding markets to sell the work in order to make a living.

CNN photojournalist Bethany Swain found herself working as a solo videojournalist, shooting, writing, and developing a half-hour continuing series called "In Focus." But she admits spending as much time selling ideas for the stories to her bosses as she does actually producing the projects. "When you put your heart and soul into a story," says Swain, "you want show producers to know so people can see it."[2]

Let's face it. Journalism is an extremely competitive field. It's a reporter's job to ferret out other peoples' information—often tidbits that those people don't want others to know. Reporters and news operations that can do that consistently better than their competition will likely have a bigger audience than their competition down the street or at another address down the Web. Reporters who consistently are enterprising in digging up information that others don't have will be valued assets in their organization—breaking more stories, getting more air time or space online, and probably moving on to the most prized jobs the profession has to offer.

For many journalists there is no better feeling than finding consequential information that has not been published before and developing that information into a well-told story that is relevant to the medium's audience. Better still is the rush one gets when the story uncovers some public malfeasance, helps nail some bad guys or warns the public of some danger or fraud.

Those are the kinds of stories that reporters dream about. Those are the kinds of stories that don't happen every day. Those are the kinds of stories that have to be pursued step-by-step, link-by-link, source-by-source by someone who cares about doing journalism in the public interest. Caring about the stories you do is the key ingredient. Former NBC *Dateline* correspondent John Larson says, "You always have to have one story you're working on that you're passionate about."[3]

Journalists are more likely to be passionate about their stories if they dig them up themselves instead of just being handed the story from an editor or assignment desk. Being an enterprising VJ means you will break stories, follow up on them, and be the journalistic expert on that issue. You will own the story from beginning to end; people will be calling you when they want your report, background information, or a panelist to discuss just how you broke the story. In developing your brand as a consistent enterpriser, you constantly increase your value as a reporter and video storyteller.

How do solo videojournalists make sure they are always enterprising stories that they are passionate about? The short answer is THINK AHEAD. Here are ten tips using that acronym as a guide that will give a VJ the tools to dig out new information and *be there before the competition to turn it into a story.*

Try to Make Friends with the Assignment Editor

This is especially important for students getting their first job in a newsroom or reporters moving into a new market or even freelancers who have to make a living selling their work to multiple organizations. Rather than flailing about trying to develop sources and come up with their own stories, novice reporters should rely at first on others who have more experience in the market. That will save new reporters time and energy, plus send a message that they are a part of the team to help the news organization.

No news organization expects new reporters to go out their first day or even first few weeks and uncover the community's long-buried secrets. Editors will send new reporters out on a variety of general assignment stories; it will likely be the assignment editor who determines whether you get the story that leads the newscast or the bottom-of-the-barrel filler that no one will remember.

So, it can pay to buddy-up to the assignment editor. Why say, "Try to make friends . . . ?" If you've ever hung around an assignment desk for more than a few minutes, you know this is the hub, the nerve center of the newsroom where the neurons are constantly clicking to feed the voracious news beast. Those who run the desk are extremely busy, taking calls, monitoring scanners, barking out orders on the phone or two-way radio.

Cultivate relationships with those who assign the stories. They have the power over your productivity. If your reel or portfolio is filled with feature stories and you need to gain more breaking news experience, let the powers-that-be know that you can finish the already assigned feature AND cover the spot news, even if you have to stay way past your normal working hours to do it. Prove your worth to the editor and the organization by turning in stellar work that exceeds expectations at every opportunity.

If you work with these folks every day, take them out to lunch, buy them a beer, and compliment their work when they deserve it. If you are a freelancer trying to increase your sales to the organization, the same tips apply. Try to make friends with these busy people and you could find your stories at the organization steadily moving to the top of the barrel—and your career along with it.

Head and Shoulders above the Rest

You're not the only one with ambition. There are others across town at the competition—and right in your own newsroom—who desire to be the best and leave you in the dust.

But as an enterpriser, you have the mindset to be even better.

There are many skills you need to acquire and master to be head and shoulders above those you are competing against. As a VJ, you need to be a good writer, understanding when to let natural sound and video speak for you. Yet you will never be a master storyteller if you don't come up with good story ideas in the first place. You need to pay attention to the world around you and mine it for the ideas that will make your story stand out from the time you pitch it to your editors.

To do that you need to do three things: read, READ, *READ.*

Staying abreast of what is happening in the world and the community is an enterprising journalist's responsibility. At the very minimum you should subscribe to and read your local daily newspaper cover to cover BEFORE you come to work. Read other regional and national newspapers online as well. Subscribe to news magazines and other special-interest magazines that will broaden your horizons.

You should also be listening to daily newscasts on the radio and TV. If you are a TV reporter, watch your network's news before coming to work; what are they covering that you could localize? What are the other local stations reporting before you come to work? What is on the radio news that day? What are the DJs talking about? Is there a preponderance of chatter on Twitter about a certain subject? Check a wide variety of Web sites and tweets to see what others are already covering.

Can you spot trends from reading, watching, and listening to these sources? You need to keep up with what is happening in the world so that your stories don't rehash the same old information. If you are following up on something already reported, your story should break new ground and move the story forward so that others will be following your lead.

If you know what's being reported already, you can avoid covering stale ground. Use others' stories as background, perhaps taking a piece of that information and focusing on it to develop a different angle. Seek answers that the prior stories left open to question. You may end up with a better story that uncovers unexpected information. Plus, you may start to see stories that no one else has even recognized as a blockbuster. But it will not happen unless you constantly pay attention to what is already being reported in a variety of media.

In the process, you may want to develop an expertise, or beat, in one or more areas: aviation, fashion, politics, or business, for example. "Today's successful reporters need to be experts on their beats, with the ability to help readers by sorting truth from spin, and the important from the trivial," writes Robert Niles in the *Online Journalism Review*.[4] Your goal is to be so well informed about the world in general and become a quasi-expert in one or more areas so that editors will call on you to develop, shoot, and write stories for their organization.

You are adding value to your VJ brand each time you do that.

Increase Your Sources

Very few stories have a "Deep Throat," the mysterious source who tips you about some flagrant misdeed. Instead, good reporters develop most stories by piecing together information from established, on-the-record sources developed through patient, hard work.

Developing these sources is important not just for reporters new to a market, but those who have been around for awhile. If you aren't increasing your sources every day, then you haven't done your job. If you work a beat, you need to develop a rapport with people you can call on to break stories on that beat. If you are a general assignment reporter, then develop sources you can call on for a sound bite or background information to tell your story.

Also use social networking tools such as Facebook or Twitter to find sources for individual stories. Crowd sourcing by using contacts on these devices may provide just the right person needed for a sound bite for a one-day story and could lead to developing long-term sources as well.

Work especially hard to develop sources who have a different ethnic background from you. You should have a list of sources to call upon not just for the occasions when a story calls for a comment from a specific ethnicity, but everyday stories should have a variety of voices from diverse groups.

Don't wait for them to call you. After you do a story you are pleased with, give your sources a call to thank them. Take those who are especially useful out for coffee. If you have an expense account, put it to use treating a valued source to lunch or dinner. Give others a call periodically just to see how things are going. Ask them if they're doing anything new—or something they've been proud to tell their families about. If you gain their trust, you might also find out about things in their job that disturb them; those could lead to good stories, too. You never know where that information and background could lead.

Your goal in developing these sources is to know something before you see it or read it on the competition.

Names and Numbers

Once you have all these sources, you need an organized method of getting their names and numbers when you need them in a hurry. Seconds count in this business; if you are the second to call a source for an interview on a breaking story, then you may see that interview on the competition's six o'clock news instead of doing the interview yourself.

In the old days a Rolodex on the desktop or a little black book to carry around helped reporters keep track of their sources. Now a variety of electronic devices keep names and numbers handy at a moment's notice. It's easy to update names on a PDA, a cell phone, or a Blackberry, find a number and call it in a matter of seconds.

Remember: when a tornado strikes a nearby town at 5:50, those seconds may make a difference in getting crucial information to your audience at six p.m. or posting the information on your Web site even earlier.

Keep a Calendar

Just as important as names and numbers is finding a way to organize your own follow-up file. Very few stories are one-shot deals; most will require at least one follow-up. Don't count on the editors to keep track of YOUR stories and remind you that an event is coming up that needs an update.

A day planner-style paper calendar is useful as a reporter's filing system. Jot down notes for a day you should call a source, or write in dates for events and even stuff news releases, paper notes, or scripts in the calendar for background.

Use that calendar—or an electronic organizer if that is more helpful—as a tickler to remind you of important events to cover and calls to make to keep up with sources and events. If a source tells you to call back to follow up on the fifteenth, jot it down in your calendar on the fifteenth AND the twelfth or thirteenth. The source may have moved up his schedule by a few days—and you would hate to see your competition break the story the morning it's marked in your calendar.

A, B, C—or Connect the Dots

After the September 11 attacks, many wondered why the U.S. intelligence community failed to connect the dots from the information already available so they could prevent the terrorists from acting.

Good enterprising VJs who are well read and have good sources also should connect the dots among various events so they can develop groundbreaking stories.

There are things happening all over the world that could be grist for a good story in your community. Why is it a story in Florida or North Carolina when William Gray speaks? He is a professor in Colorado, but perhaps has his greatest impact on millions of people living in eastern coastal states. He is the expert who makes annual predictions on the number of hurricanes and tropical storms. So what he says is newsworthy and might be turned into a story from Bangor to Key West and Jacksonville to Galveston.

There are many ways to connect the dots to make good local stories. If Congress passes a new tax bill, how will that affect people in your community? Now that you have been increasing sources and have a good way to keep track of them, you can get that key interview for the ten o'clock news when the Senate passes the bill at 8:30. When a major event sends tidal waves through the media world will you be ready to catch the wave and beat the competition with your sources?

Now that you are well read, you might also conceive of angles that others have missed; work those angles and sources into a story that will be memorable and leave the competition wondering how did we miss that?

History: Know It and *Predict the Future*

Let's say your editor sends you to cover the announcement that John Doe is running for Congress. Since you've been keeping up on the news, you know the right questions to ask: will the president's tax cut help or hurt the economy? How do you stand on privatizing Social Security? What should the United States do about the threat of terrorism?

Those are all legitimate questions for a congressional candidate. But what if a background check reveals that Doe had been convicted of child molestation twenty-five years ago? That bit of history should have changed your line of questioning.

History does make a difference in the stories we tell. Updating history can be a story in itself. Virtually every news organization around the country does anniversary stories. For example, the anniversaries of September 11 will merit updates for decades to come.

VJs can get a fresh perspective on great historical events from those who lived through them. Indeed, each year countless news organizations do Pearl Harbor anniversary stories because the event still resonates with passion today and has a new context in light of the terrorist attacks in 2001.

The bombing at Hiroshima changed people for all time. Perhaps the angle on that next August 6 anniversary would demonstrate how lives are different now because of atomic weapons. Or an enterprising VJ might use the date as a news peg to explore a world with nuclear devices in the hands of a rogue nation or terrorist group.

The point is there are a myriad of good stories to tell about people based on how history has affected their lives. History can be important fodder for any news organization. Using history to help *predict the future* can set the VJ apart from the rest of the news pack:

A tornado will strike somewhere in Oklahoma.

A hurricane will blow ashore in Louisiana.

A brush fire will inflame California.

Enterprising journalists don't know when. They don't know where exactly. But based on the history of those locations, an enterprising VJ can predict that those places will face such events again. The challenge for journalists is to be prepared to cover them as quickly and accurately as possible when they do happen.

Every credible news organization is planning for major events in the future whether it is the Olympics, elections, or a disaster that has not yet arrived. Enterprising journalists can use their knowledge of history to predict a number of things that are likely to happen and prepare to cover them in a way that will stand out from the competition.

Eyes and Ears—Keep Them Open

Your powers of observation can help you recognize stories that might slip by others: What are people talking about in the checkout line at the grocery? Why does that newly paved road already have potholes? Does there seem to be an increase in credit come-ons in the mail?

Trends don't happen all at once; you may see the first piece of a puzzle one day and see another piece a few days or weeks later. Now that you've started connecting the dots, you can see how seemingly random events may actually be related. You can be the first to connect those dots and develop a story showing how they have an impact on your audience.

Let's examine those potholes in the road a bit more. You saw the contractor paving the highway a few months ago. That's usually no big deal unless the road had been controversial as a killer highway, had been a major inconvenience to drivers, or officials had debated how much they need to spend on the repairs. If so, you may have done a story about it.

But a few months later when you begin to see potholes developing in the new pavement, as an enterprising VJ, you begin to ask: Why? What causes potholes to develop in a brand-new surface? Is the public agency responsible for this taking any action to correct the situation? How much will it cost to fix them? Is anyone being held responsible?

Perhaps the questions lead you to substandard materials the contractor used: the repair might cost taxpayers millions more. Or it might also lead to a contractor who is the county commissioner's cousin or campaign contributor. Was the job a payback in some way?

Either scenario could be a groundbreaking story with high public interest that will leave the competition scrambling to catch up. And it all started simply because of some questions from an enterprising journalist's powers of observation about something that others might see as routine or mundane.

Dozens of similar situations are happening in communities everywhere. They are just waiting on an enterprising reporter to connect the dots and start asking the right questions.

If you do keep your eyes and ears open, you never know when a story will strike. Once I was waiting to interview an environmental official about a routine topic. The receptionist asked if I was there about the *radioactive* water. I said no, but made sure I asked the official about it when I interviewed him. It was too late in the day to develop the story, but I went back the next day for a formal interview. I broke the story about a mobile home park where people had to drink bottled water because their wells were contaminated by naturally occurring radioactivity.

That became a continuing story as other communities relying on wells began checking their water to see if it was safe. But I was well ahead of the curve. I owned the story from the beginning, breaking new angles nearly every day. No one at other stations could catch up and even local newspapers were quoting my stories on the radioactive water problems.

That was one of those feel-good journalistic moments, where publicizing the issue led to awareness about a public health concern. And it all started from an innocuous comment too good to ignore.

Allow Your Instincts to Work—or
More Poetically—Follow Your Heart

When I was just out of college I worked as a reporter at a small-town radio station. I went to cover a traffic accident at a local school. A man had a heart attack while driving; he plowed through a four-way stop sign, somehow missed all of the cars in the parking lot before smashing into a plate-glass window in a kindergarten class. One child died and a dozen others were seriously injured.

After covering that tragedy I started asking myself how such an accident could happen: if there is a God, I asked myself, then how could he let it happen?

It was a question that wouldn't let me go. Every day I pondered the fate of those children and how such a thing could have happened to them. The questions led me to begin researching a story. There had been accidents in other cities in which drivers had heart attacks and ran down pedestrians on sidewalks; in my community a county commissioner recently had pulled over to the side of the road while driving and died of a heart attack.

I began calling motor vehicle officials in the state as well as traffic safety experts around the country. There were laws to prevent epileptics from driving until they were certified as safe to drive—but none for people with heart conditions.

I gathered a lot of information, but I still didn't have what I needed to tell the story.

Then, as luck would have it, the governor came to town; I asked him all the standard questions about the newsworthy topics of the day. Then I asked him about the information I had discovered concerning drivers having heart attacks. The governor, who had been a physician before going into politics, said the state should do something to make sure drivers with heart conditions don't become deadly menaces.

With those few comments from the state's top official, I now had my story, one that later won an award. But that wasn't the best part to me. Researching, probing, and doing the story had wrestled the demon out of my system; I couldn't do much to help those kids injured or killed in that school accident, but I did what I could as a journalist to call attention to the problem and perhaps prevent a similar tragedy from taking place again.

I followed my heart and used my journalistic instincts to develop and report a story that no one else had. The lesson I learned was that when something is nagging at you, don't shove it aside. If something doesn't sound right, keep asking questions about it until you are satisfied. When something doesn't make sense, find out why. If it troubles you, it will likely concern others.

Allow your instincts to work; follow your heart; turn your nagging questions into a story.

Don't Procrastinate

There's a lot of wasted time in newsrooms. We chat with one another, yak about the competition, and kibitz about sports teams. Some of that is valuable in building newsroom camaraderie, but a lot of that time could be put to better use enterprising stories.

Take some of that time to call a source about next week's event; make a call to nail down an elusive fact for today's story; call someone to see why that newly paved road does have potholes.

No one gave me extra time to do the research on the heart attack story. Over a couple of weeks I pieced together the information between all my other daily assignments. When the governor came to town I was ready.

Just as important, don't give up when it seems the odds are against you. "Do not be easily intimidated or deterred. Be tough," former CBS and CNN correspondent Deborah Potter told graduating journalism students. "Great journalists need to be courageous, to get past the obstacles thrown in their way and to tell stories people may not want to hear."[5]

Stick to your guns. Make time work for you instead of against you. If you procrastinate, or give up, you are giving all those other enterprising VJs the edge.

The bottom line is THINK AHEAD. Your career could depend on it.

Be Ready for the Future

A survey of 2009 recently employed mass communication college graduates showed that 14.6 percent of them were producing video in some capacity. That was an increase from 8.1 percent just three years before—or a jump in video jobs for new graduates of 80 percent even in a down economy in which the overall job market had deteriorated substantially.[6] If you have the skills to be a videojournalist, you can continue to tap into the rising video trend, though it may have to be in a job-hopping kind of career.

Enterprising VJs will always have to deal with a changing media landscape. For example, one outlet for VJs, the American News Project, merged with the *Huffington Post* Investigative Fund in 2009, but still is a valuable outlet for quality videojournalism.[7]

In England, one media veteran in announcing his departure from the Telegraph Media Group declared, "The future is individual journalists, not big media." Greg Hadfield went on to say that journalists will need more entrepreneurial skills to survive in the future. "The future is much more diverse. There's not a dichotomy between being a journalist and an entrepreneur—the future is the individual journalist, not big media."[8]

Market Yourself for the Future

VJs need to be prepared for a freelance career or one in whatever remains of the "big media." Amy Gahran, whose career has taken her from freelance journalist to media consultant to online news editor, says, "Develop your radar for spotting an opportunity and having the initiative and the assertiveness to go after it."[9] For freelance solo videojournalists, outlets for their work already exist on the Internet through YouTube or its rival, Vimeo.

In the future it will be easier and commonplace to find news video on all kinds of devices that we carry around. Consumer product researcher James L. McQuivey predicts that along with our TVs, cell phones, and computers, by 2013 alarm clocks, GPS devices, gas stations, and taxis will be able to stream video in a world that he calls "OmniVideo."[10] Some organizations are already utilizing cell phones for multimedia journalists to stream video and produce clandestinely shot videojournalism pieces or what are called "snatched interviews."[11]

At WFOR, the CBS affiliate in Miami, investigative producer Gio Benitez was one of the first to shoot video for a story with an iPhone. "As people walked by my edit suite and looked at the video," he writes, "they thought it was shot with one of our more 'professional' cameras."[12]

Whether the technologies change or the personnel running them, a successful VJ must be able to keep up with those changes. At WTSP-TV in St. Petersburg, Florida, backpack journalist Janie Porter says she went through seven changes to her workflow as the equipment evolved. Since she is not a "tech" person, she says "keeping on top of the changes is a big challenge for me."[13]

Once you decide to keep current with the technology, you will need to tailor your pitches to use those skills for your target media. Whether you are pitching your stories for a multimedia presentation for a newspaper Web site, using Skype to do a solo live shot for a TV station, or making a quick video for a mobile phone service, keep coming up with ideas and that will help you build value in the organization. Lynn French, a backpack journalist at KPNX-TV in Phoenix, believes that VJs who come to their news meetings with their own ideas have more control over their destinies. "By the sheer act of pitching stories," she writes, "you will build your brand as a contributor."[14]

One VJ who has learned well the traits of an enterprising reporter is Mara Schiavocampo. She has been recognized as the Emerging Journalist of the Year by the National Association of Black Journalists and won an award for TV reporting from the Society of Environmental Journalists.[15]

She left a position as an anchor and reporter at RNN, a New York cable news operation, in 2005 to strike out on her own as a freelance VJ. Her trademark is finding stories that others have overlooked. For example, her SEJ winner, "When the Beaches Turned Black," took place in Beirut, Lebanon; while other journalists focused on the fighting on shore, Schiavocampo focused her camera on the enviornmental destruction of a giant oil spill offshore. "My currency, I've realized, is always going to be in my ideas, because [news organizations] have the resources and the people to execute anything they can think of," she says. "But if they don't think of it, then it's mine for the taking."[16]

As Schiavocampo has discovered, enterprise reporting skills are a key to success and recognition in journalism. Her enterprising led to a job with NBC News.

Enterprising Skills Are Marketing Skills

Once a VJ has started utilizing the THINK AHEAD principles to enhance their reporting, he or she must still use enterprising skills in selling their stories as well as promoting themselves.

The downsizing of mainstream media means there may be fewer staff positions in newspaper and television newsrooms. Yet there are new media opportunities for solo videojournalists at nearly every mouse click. Many VJs will have to work as freelancers, so there may not be a check coming in every pay period.

There are ways, however, to ensure a steady income and make a living as a VJ. Media consultant Terry Heaton says in the future there will be more journalists leaving mainstream media to work independently, perhaps even arranging advertising for their own product. "The future begins with a fundamental belief that journalists, professional or otherwise," he writes, "will be independent contractors, building individual brands based on the quality —and popularity—of their work."[17]

One freelancing site is *True/Slant*. The Web site offers journalists opportunities to blog and post video. The journalists receive some sort of compensation, whether from the site, or advertising they solicit themselves. "It's tailored for the entrepreneurial journalist," says founder Lewis Dvorkin. "We're enabling and empowering journalists to develop their own brand."[18]

One journalist taking advantage of True/Slant is ABC's Claire Shipman, who is using it to promote a book she co-wrote. "We are looking to start a conversation," Shipman says, "and in this new Internet world, you really have to branch out and put your tentacles in a million different places."[19]

To take advantage of the freelance market, the Travel Channel has been training independent videojournalists at its own Travel Academy. The budding travel VJs learn to shoot and edit videos. Besides figuring out how to produce their own travel stories, those who attend the classes, which the students pay for, make contacts that may help them sell their work to the cable channel. Former Travel Channel president Pat Younge told one class that those contacts could be the start of a continuing working relationship: "If you do something that works, we'll want to do something else with you," he told the wannabe travel VJs.[20]

Don't Be Shy about Promoting Your Brand

Since more VJs will likely be working as freelancers, there's an old phrase they need to adopt: "If you don't promote yourself, who will?" Let's face it: in an information marketplace where TV, text, video, blogs, cell phones, and podcasts are all competing for viewers' attention, it is no time to be shy.

So enterprising solo videojournalists have to be ready to market themselves, promote their product, and extol their brand. Photojournalism and video-journalism educator Ken Kobré writes, "As with writing and still photography, making a living—or even a dime—from VJ projects will require hustle, moxie, and good old-fashioned marketing and self-promotion."[21]

There are abundant social media sites for entrepreneurial solo videojournalists to make contacts—both sources and clients. These sites, such as Facebook, Twitter, and LinkedIn, help journalists promote their work and ultimately create a brand that stands out in a crowded field.[22]

"Look ahead and start to think strategically about where media is going and about where your interests and passions lie," says Amy Gahran. "And make sure you are creating content and putting it online about that right now, because then people who have opportunities or are potential partners or potential clients will find you for the kind of stuff that you want to be doing."[23]

These are some basic things VJs need to do to be successful at the business of telling and selling video stories:

- Have business cards made and always hand them out.
- Define the market for your stories: Web, TV, podcasts, etc.
- Develop one or two consistent outlets that pay for your stories.
- Have extra content for the Web besides your video story.
- Establish your own Web site with video and links to those you work for.
- Blog about your VJ activities.
- Use social networking Web sites to promote your work.
- Notify interested viewers by e-mail and Twitter about upcoming stories.
- Experiment with the latest technology for video storytelling.
- Spend some time each day marketing yourself.
- Join professional organizations for networking and knowledge.
- Enter professional contests for recognition.
- Write "how to" articles for professional publications or Web sites.
- Make yourself available for professional panel discussions.
- Utilize the THINK AHEAD principles as business tools.

Last, but certainly not least, don't get discouraged. Establishing yourself as a premier VJ does not happen overnight or even after a few weeks. It takes long, hard work to build a brand that people recognize and will call on when needed. You have to be willing to put in the time and effort to do that.

"The most important thing at the end of the day," ABC correspondent and anchor Elizabeth Vargas says, "is to love what you do, and remember that it's the slow and steady pace that wins the race."[24]

Discussion and VJ Exercise

1. Make a list of media you should be reading, watching, or listening to every day to make sure you are well informed and up-to-date with the news in your community. Now add five more media outlets to that list that have areas of specialization that interest you.
2. Who is the gatekeeper for stories for a news organization that you work for or would like to sell a story to? How can you "make friends" with that person to make sure you can get good story assignments?
3. Have you ever procrastinated and as a result found that someone beat you on something you set as a goal to accomplish? What was it? How could you have better utilized your time to make sure that you got to the goal first?
4. What type of system do you have of keeping track of sources? Is it useful enough that you can find their contact information within thirty seconds? How do you track stories that you need to follow up? Is there a better way to organize that? Then why not do it?
5. Make a prediction about something that you think will happen in your community. How can you justify the prediction? Do you know specifics about when or where this prediction will occur? What is your plan to cover this in the future?
6. Draw up a plan to market yourself. If you are employed by an organization what things do you need to do to sell yourself to be either recognized or promoted within the organization?
7. If you are freelancer, (a) make a list of places you would like to sell your stories, and (b) make a list of the tools you need to develop—e.g., starting a Twitter account, or making a better source list—to move forward as a VJ to sell more of your stories to your targeted organizations.
8. Think ahead twenty years. What will the market for news media be like then? What technologies might develop in that time for video news? What are you doing to prepare yourself to be competitive in that marketplace?

Chapter 11 Focus
Enterprising Every Day

Al Tompkins is an award-winning former TV reporter and news director. Now he is the Broadcast/Online Group Leader at Poynter Institute, a journalism think tank and training site in St. Petersburg, Florida. One of his trademarks is *Al's Morning Meeting,* which he puts on Poynter's Web site every day to help journalists develop story ideas. Tompkins bills the site as "Story ideas that you can localize and enterprise. Posted by 7:30 a.m. Mon-Fri." [1]

Tompkins answered these questions by e-mail: [2]

Q. How do you define enterprising journalism?

A. Find me something I don't know. An enterprising journalist is one who goes out looking for something beyond "what" happened to discover the "why, how, and where else" of the story.

Anybody can tell me what happened, they can tell me basic facts, but it takes a journalist to explain the facts in context and to discover characters who can deliver the information in a meaningful way.

Q. Why is it important to be an enterpriser as a journalist?

A. I can get INFORMATION in a lot of ways, on my cell phone, from cable TV, radio, online. They even have gas pumps that stream news, stock tickers, and sports scores now. So the days when the newscast could just tell me WHAT is happening are long gone. I need you to tell me something I don't know or there is no reason for me to give you my time. You have to assume now that the viewer knows WHAT happened today when they sit down to watch your show. The rare exception is the breaking story that actually develops in front of you live. Those, actually, are fairly rare.

Increasingly, nonjournalists are discovering information. Let's not just hand over the franchise to nonjournalists, let's get out and discover some things ourselves. And let's take a look at what the nonjournalists ("citizen journalists" they often call themselves) have discovered and see what we can do with that information.

I find that journalists often use the same old sources, take the same routes home, eat at the same place every day. To discover new things about your community, you have to constantly experience it in new ways, meet new people, learn new things. Bowling leagues are a great way to meet ordinary people. So are summertime Little League games and senior citizen centers. When is the last time you dropped by a feed mill to see what farmers are talking about or just went to the corner cafe to sit and listen to the chatter? Journalists rarely drop by the gun shop unless they are doing stories.

Read new things. Every time I travel, and that is just about every week, I pick up a magazine that I ordinarily might not read. From *Ebony* to *Ladies Home Journal* to *Gun and Ammo,* I want to know what is a hot topic for these folks.

Q. At what time do you begin preparing *Al's Morning Meeting*? What materials do you use to come up with ideas?

A. I never stop. It is something I work on all day every day. I use all sorts of things including newspapers big and small, RSS feeds, most popular and most e-mailed lists from lots of Web sites from NPR to the *Wall Street Journal* to regional and small newspapers and broadcast stations. Lots of my readers send me things they think I might like. I listen for stories all the time and carry a piece of paper with me to write down ideas when I hear them. The page I have in my pocket now has three ideas on it I will work on for tomorrow.

Q. What techniques or tips can you give journalists to help them develop their own story ideas?

A. Read more—and not the stuff you want to read but the stuff you usually don't read.

Get to know more people who have their pulse on the community. When I was a street reporter I had a preschool teacher, a junkyard operator, a priest who ran a homeless shelter, a pharmacist, a veterinarian, a doctor, a grocery store owner, a hardware store owner, a tailor and a coin shop owner who were all close sources. I never put any of them on TV—but they were all people who heard a lot. They would sometimes call me but they always took my call or would see me if I dropped in. If I wanted to know what was happening in the business world, I needed to talk with a businessperson. If I wanted to know what was happening on the street, I needed somebody whose life it is to know such things.

Of course the cops and lawyers and judges will all be good sources, but make sure you get to know ordinary folks too.

Q. As more stations and newspapers turn to solo videojournalists to cover the news, are there any enterprising tips you can offer that would help them stand out from competitors, either two-person TV crews or the traditional pen-and-paper reporter?

A. Do what others can't. The one big advantage of a one-person crew is you are not so imposing. People might talk with you because you are not mister high-and-mighty reporterman in a suit and tie. I would wear a lav [lavaliere] mic when shooting so that you can also narrate while you shoot if the opportunity arises to do so. Let the viewer know that you are both reporter and photographer by letting the viewer look through your lens as if they are looking through your eye. I would try first-person reporting if I was working alone as a franchise.

Q.What do you see as the future for solo videojournalists in twenty-first-century media?

A.No question more folks will be working alone as gear gets lighter and budgets get tighter. It is not always a good thing. Sometimes this is a dangerous craft and you need a companion to protect you. Sometimes stories are really complicated or logistically challenging. You need people to help with setup, to fetch interviews and information or work through logistics of shooting. It is darn hard to do that sometimes.

When you are working alone, it can be hard to find the people you need to interview, covering trials is the worst because you can't have your camera in the courtroom but you have to be in the courtroom to hear testimony. Newsrooms need to set reasonable expectations for what one person can do in the field.

Glossary

APJ—all platform journalist. A term coined by CNN to describe its solo videojournalists who must provide material both for cable TV programs and the organization's Web site.

Back light—one of the lights used in a normal three-light setup for an interview. The back light is placed opposite the key light. It helps set the subject away from the background and can provide an interesting lighting effect on the subject's head. See also Fill light and Key light.

Backlight—light coming from behind a subject that creates a harsh shadow on the side toward the camera. It is normally something to avoid unless you want to silhouette a person who wants to remain anonymous.

B-roll—also cover video. An old film term, it is raw video a news camera crew shoots to illustrate a story. They will edit several minutes of b-roll down to 1:15 or a 1:30 for a package.

Backpack journalist—a term for solo videojournalists used by many Gannett stations.

Bite—short for sound bite.

Bounce light—a lighting technique used when a VJ has only one artificial light. It creates a more normal-looking lighting scheme by bouncing the light off a ceiling or other object to reduce the harsh shadows that appear when the light is directed straight at the subject.

BPJ—backpack journalist.

Cinema vérité—a motion picture term. In videojournalism it refers to a style of telling a story that relies on the video and sound to convey realism.

Close-up—a tight shot. Part of a sequence of shooting video.

Continuity—the act of editing a series of images that flow from one to the other and make sense in the progression of the story.

Cover video—raw video a VJ shoots to illustrate a story. The VJ edits several minutes of cover video down to 1:15 or a 1:30 for a package.

Crossing the axis—an imaginary 180-degree line. When a two shot and reverse shot are cut together, they should not cross the axis or it might confuse viewers.

Cut—a term used by video editors to indicate one shot edited directly to another without a dissolve or other special effect.

Cutaway—a shot showing some logical action in a sequence of video to avoid a jump cut. In a sequence of someone working at the computer, you could start with a medium shot (MS) of the person at the computer looking left, then use a shot of his hands, then a sound bite of him looking right. That shot of the hands is a cutaway, which avoids the appearance of the person's head "jumping" from left to right if the MS and sound bite were edited back to back.

Cut in—a close-up of something previously seen in a wide shot or medium shot. Sometimes used in a standup to draw attention to an object the reporter is holding or demonstrating.

Depth of field—in a photograph or video, the range of the image that is in focus or has acceptable sharpness.

Digital correspondent—KGTV in San Diego uses solo videojournalists to cover stories, but calls them digital correspondents.

Dissolve—a transitional effect. It blends or fades one shot into another. It can be used to make jump cuts less distracting or make a transition to a new scene.

Emmy—an award given for excellence in a number of different categories by the Academy of Television Arts and Sciences.

ENG—electronic news gathering. Many TV stations switched from film to this form of recording moving images (video) on tape in the 1970s.

Enterprise reporting—the concept of reporters consistently breaking stories that have been unreported before.

Fill light—one of the lights used in a normal three-light setup for an interview. Along with the key light, the fill light is placed on the front of the subject, but each on a different side of the interviewee. The fill light is less intense than the key light and helps fill in some shadows created by the key. See also Back light and Key light.

Film—the earliest method of capturing moving images for TV news was on celluloid film, usually 16 millimeter with various sound recording methods.

Flash frame—in an edited video story, one frame that is between others that does not match the rest. It causes an instantaneous flash that is distracting.

Focus—the act of turning the focus ring on a lens. Or, the portion of an image that is sharp; i.e., in focus. Another use of the term is the story focus, which deals with how well the story stays on track with its main point or theme.

Hyperlocal—a news coverage strategy that focuses on the neighborhood level rather than a metropolitan or region-wide audience.

Into and out of frame—a videography technique when someone or something enters the frame and then goes out of frame. The shot may use just one of the techniques; i.e., out of frame and not into frame. It is useful in editing to avoid jump cuts.

Iris—a diaphragm that expands or contracts to control the amount of light coming into a camera lens.

Jump cut—two shots, edited back to back, that do not make visual sense. An example is a medium shot of a speaker at a podium while she is wearing glasses. The second shot is a close-up of her without glasses. A cutaway or dissolve is needed to avoid a jump cut.

Key light—one of the lights used in a normal three-light setup for an interview. The key light is the light that provides the main illumination of the subject. The harsh shadows created by the key are balanced with two other lights, the fill light and the back light.

Lavaliere—a small microphone that attaches to an interviewee's shirt.

Live shot—in television newscasts, the reporter is actually reporting from the scene as it happens live. The reporter may tell the story by talking while "live" or also pitch to prerecorded video such as a package.

Medium shot—halfway between a close-up and a wide shot in the focal length of a zoom lens. Also a shot that shows a subject that half fills the screen instead of showing the full perspective of the subject in a wide shot or a detailed image in a close-up. Abbreviated as MS.

MoJo—mobile journalist. This term is often used to refer to newspaper reporters who take a camera and shoot video with it, then feed it back to the newsroom by Wi-Fi.

Multimedia—shorthand for multiple media. Often used for organizations that produce news for more than one medium as well as using multiple elements, such as audio, photos, and graphics, in storytelling.

Multimedia journalist—a term for solo videojournalists used by KUSA in Washington, D.C.

Natural sound—also called nat/snd or wild sound. It is the sound the camera picks up that takes place while shooting cover video. Natural sound is one of the video storytelling tools that helps deliver an experience to the audience. It is different from the interview sound, though interviews may also be conducted with the camera's natural sound microphone.

Nat/snd—abbreviation for natural sound.

Noise—see Natural sound. Noise is different than natural sound. Noise may be captured by a camera but is not a sound that helps in telling a story. It is a distraction if used in an edited story.

Nonlinear editing—video editing with a computer. In tape editing, the video has to be laid down sequentially from point A to point Z, a linear type of editing. In computer editing, the video can be laid down in any order and rearranged at any time, hence its nonlinear nature.

NPPA—National Press Photographers Association. A professional group of both still and video news photographers.

One-man band—the original term for TV reporter-photographers who worked alone to cover stories. Many reporters and photographers got their start in TV news as one-man bands. It has fallen into disfavor because the term ignores many women who also work alone as reporter-photographers. Plus the term one-man band is seen as a mere cost-cutting measure instead of a model of coverage that utilizes the advantages of solo videojournalism to provide increased and different coverage of stories at a lower cost.

Pacing—a reference to the speed at which an edited video story unfolds.

Package—often abbreviated as PKG, it is the story form in which an anchor in the studio introduces a reporter. Then a video begins with the reporter's story narration—along with video, natural sound, and sound bites.

Pan—a horizontal movement of the camera while recording video.

Peabody—one of broadcasting's top awards, given by the University of Georgia.

Pitch—the act of making or writing a story idea that one will try to sell an editor on doing.

Platypus—an organization that trains mostly still photojournalists in the art of videojournalism.

Production values—the technical requirements needed in good videography such as audio, exposure, and focus among others.

Pulitzer Prize—one of the top prizes awarded to print journalists.

Rack focus—the act of changing the focus while recording video. Also a shot using the rack focus technique in a story to direct attention from one object to another in the edited video.

Reverse shot—a shot from behind an interview subject looking at the interviewer. Used to cover a jump cut in an interview.

Rosenblum model—A VJ covering a story, usually about one person or event. Working alone, with a lightweight, small camera, the VJ should be able to develop a rapport with sources that a two-person crew might not be able to develop. The Rosenblum model does not use a reporter stand-up or a live shot that seems to focus more on the reporter than the story.

RTDNA—Radio Television Digital News Association. Changed its name from RTNDA in 2009.

RTNDA—Radio Television News Directors Association. Changed its name to RTDNA, Radio Television Digital News Association in 2009.

Sequence—a series of shots taken of the same scene to help edit the story so it flows smoothly. A typical sequence is a WS, MS, CU. When cut together, the WS would set up the scene, the MS would move us closer to the action, and the CU would get us up close to the subject. A sequence, however, could be in any order: MS, CU, WS or CU, WS, MS. Once edited, the sequence should flow without jump cuts to match action between each shot.

Shotgun mic—a highly directional microphone that is often mounted on top of a camera to get natural sound while recording video. It also can be dismounted from the camera to use in interviews.

Solo videojournalism—the art of one person doing the reporting, shooting, writing, and editing for a video story. A person who does this is called a VJ. Some of the duties are similar to those working as one-man bands, but proponents of solo videojournalism see VJing as a better way to approach stories since it emphasizes the ability of the VJ with a small camera to get up close to people and have full control of the creative aspects of storytelling.

SoJo—solo journalist. Same as solo videojournalist.

Sound bite—A segment of a recorded interview used in a story.

Sound overlap—a video editing technique in which the sound precedes the video associated with it. In the edited version, the viewer hears the sound from the scene first, then the video that goes with the sound appears a few seconds later.

Standup—in a package, a prerecorded segment with the reporter appearing on camera to narrate part of the story. This is not a live shot, which is the reporter at the scene, but is not prerecorded.

Steady Bag—a flexible bag filled with beans or sand that videographers use to support a camera to maintain a steady image when not shooting from a tripod. Also the brand name of a product.

Stop—an f-stop. It is the iris control on a camera lens that lets in less or more light. Typically the f-stop on a lens will be fully open at about f-2 to almost closed at f-16 or f-22. Videographers and photographers use the term "stop down" to contract the iris to let in less light.

Super—short for superimposition. It is usually the lower third graphic used to identify people or locations.

Tilt—a vertical movement of the camera while recording video.

Time code—time of the tape or digital media that is embedded in the video and will not change, even if one hits the time reset button. This is useful in logging and editing because the time code is the same when played in any machine.

Timeline—the portion of the nonlinear editor used to control the placement and order of video and audio for creating a story.

Two shot—in a studio, this is a camera shot in which two anchors appear side-by-side. In field interviews recorded on tape, this is a shot where we see the reporter and interview subject together—usually shot over the shoulder of the reporter.

Video—the electronic recording of moving images.

Videography—the art of recording moving images on video.

Videojournalism—the art of telling reality-based stories using videography techniques. Some use the term with two words, video journalism. This book, however, adheres to the use of a one-word term, as in photojournalism.

Videojournalist—a person who practices the art of videojournalism. It has a wider meaning than solo videojournalist or VJ, however. A reporter and videographer in a two-person crew are both videojournalists—just as a VJ working alone is a videojournalist.

Viewfinder—the part of the camera that flips out allowing the videographer to view the image being produced. The viewfinder is viewable from a short distance and is different from the camera's eyepiece, which the videographer must use by pressing his or her eye into a rubber cup to see an image.

VJ—solo videojournalist.

Vo/Sot—a story used in television newscasts that is read live by an anchor. It has voice-over video that leads into a sound bite.

Web—the World Wide Web.

White balance—this is the process of making sure that the camera registers colors properly. By setting the white balance, the camera will correctly adjust the color temperature for a white object, such as a white card carried for that purpose. Then the camera will adjust to black, the absence of colors, and register all other colors according to the light that is in use at the time. The white balance will need to be changed each time the lighting source changes, such as moving from sunlight to an indoor lighting setup. Even sunlight at different times of day, such as noon and sunset, have different color temperatures, so the camera's white balance will have to be adjusted as that lighting changes.

Wide shot—a wide shot is shot with the camera's lens set at its widest focal length and is used to give viewers an overall perspective of a scene. Sometimes called an establishing shot.

Wireless mic—a microphone that transmits its audio signal through the air, without cables to a receiver that is normally attached to and plugged into the camera.

Zebra stripes—a video camera mechanism that when engaged shows "hot spots" or areas in the frame that are overexposed or too light. The VJ should consult the camera manual to use this device properly.

Zoom—the device on a camera lens that allows the videographer to change the focal length of the image; i.e., from a wide shot to a close-up. It also describes a shot taken while using the zoom feature of the lens.

Notes

Chapter 1

1. "Like Never Before, Inauguration Experienced Online," Associated Press, Jan. 21, 2009, http://nab365bdmetrics.com//NST-2–50174767/Like-Never-Before-Inauguration-Experienced-Online.aspx, accessed Jan. 21, 2009.

2. "Zogby Poll: 67% View Traditional Journalism as 'Out of Touch,'" Zogby Poll, Feb. 27, 2008, www.zogby.com/news/ReadNews.dbm?ID=1454, accessed Mar. 4, 2008.

3. Author's telephone interview with Dirck Halstead, June 19, 2008.

4. Lewis Lazare, "TV set for ad dive," *Chicago Sun Times,* Nov. 13, 2008, www.sun-times.com/business/lazare/1277060.CST-FIN-lew13.article#, accessed Nov. 17, 2008.

5. Richard Perez-Pena, "Big News in Washington, but Far Fewer Cover It," *New York Times,* Dec. 18, 2008, 1.

6. Brian Stelter, "TV News Winds Down Operations on Iraq War," *New York Times,* Dec. 28, 2008, www.nytimes.com/2008/12/29/business/media/29bureaus.html?_r=1&scp=2&sq=nbc%20iraq&st=cse, accessed Jan. 7, 2009.

7. Paul J. Gough, "ABC Opening one-man foreign bureaus," Reuters, Oct. 3, 2007, via Yahoo Web: http://news.yahoo.com/s/nm/20071003/tv_nm/abcnews_dc_1;_ylt=Ao2e SJdBdmolQE7tWAXepOAE1vAI, accessed Nov. 8, 2007.

8. Marisa Guthrie, "ABC News Adds Four Domestic Digital Journalists," *Broadcasting and Cable,* June 3, 2009, www.broadcastingcable.com/article/278082-ABC_News_Adds_Four_Domestic_Digital_Journalists.php, accessed June 9, 2009.

9. Felix Gillette, "CBS News Hires Digital Journalist to Be Based in Afghanistan," *New York Observer,* July 27, 2009, http://www.observer.com/2009/media/cbs-news-hires-digital-journalist-be-based-afghanistan, accessed July 28, 2009.

10. "Internet Overtakes Newspaper As News Outlet," Pew Research Center for the People & the Press, Dec. 23, 2008, http://people-press.org/report/479/internet-overtakes-newspapers-a-news-outlet, accessed Jan. 16, 2009. Television news viewers declined from 74 percent in 2007 to 70 percent in 2008.

11. Lymari Morales, "Cable, Internet News Sources Growing in Popularity," Dec. 15, 2008, www.gallup.com/poll/113314/Cable-Internet-News-Sources-Growing-Popularity. aspx, accessed Dec. 16, 2008.

12. Michael Starr, "Local Motion," *New York Post,* Jan. 13, 2009, www.nypost.com/ seven/01132009/tv/local_motion_149928.htm, accessed Jan. 14, 2009.

13. Felix Gillette, "A Better News Division, Rockefeller Money Can't Buy," *New York Observer,* Oct. 21, 2008, *www.observer.com/2008/media/better-news-division-rockefeller-money-can-t-buy,* accessed Oct. 23, 2008.

14. David F. Diamond, "Jacks-of-all-trades blend four salaries into one," *Memphis Commercial Appeal,* Dec. 27, 2008, www.commercialappeal.com/news/2008/dec/27/ one-man-bands-save-tv-stations/, accessed Dec. 27, 2008.

15. Eric Deggans, "The Feed," *St. Petersburg Times,* May 12, 2009, http://blogs.tampabay. com/media/2009/05/wtspch-10-confirms-dave-wirth-will-take-over-as-stations-lead-sports-anchor.html, accessed May 12, 2009.

16. The Radio Television News Directors Association (RTNDA) changed its name to Radio Television Digital News Association (RTDNA) on Oct. 12, 2009. The author uses both names in this chapter depending on whether the citation came before or after the name change.

17. Bob Papper, "One Man Bands 2010 Update," RTDNA/Hofstra University Survey, 2010, http://www.rtdna.org/media/onemanband.pdf, accessed July 20, 2010.

18. Interview with Patti Dennis by author, Aug. 3, 2007.

19. "Gannett Out to Re-Engineer its Stations," *TVNewsDay,* Feb. 19, 2008, www. tvnewsday.com/articles/2008/02/19/daily.4, accessed Feb. 20, 2008.

20. Scott Wycoff, "Reinventing the Radio Reporter for the Digital Age," *RTNDA Communicator,* Nov./Dec. 2008, vol. 62, no. 8, 19.

21. "Backpack Journalism," *Quill,* Mar. 2008, vol. 96, no. 2, 3.

22. John Booth, "Nothing plain about changes at *Plain Dealer;* More sharing of staff, resources in works as daily continues its web, print balancing act," *Crain's Cleveland Business,* Sept. 1, 2008, www.crainscleveland.com/articld/20080901/FREE/309019948, accessed Oct. 29, 2008.

23. Emma Heald, "US: Newspapers competing with broadcast for TV awards," Dec. 16, 2008, www.editorsweblog.org/multimedia/2008/12/us_newspapers_competing_with_broadcast_f.php, accessed Dec. 16, 2008.

24. Harry Jaffe, "Reporters as Shooters—the Newest new Journalism Arrives at the Washington Post," *Washingtonian,* June 19, 2006, www.washingtonian.com/articles/ people/2242.html, accessed June 20, 2006.

25. Kelsey Blodget, "Wall Street Journal Trains Reporters to Produce Online Video," Beet.TV, Oct. 20, 2008, www.beet.tv/2008/10/wsj-reporters-p.html, accessed Oct. 24, 2008.

26. Ibid. Online video interview with Murray on Beet.TV.

27. Michael Calderone, "WaPo cuts several positions," *POLITICO,* Nov. 20, 2009, www.politico.com/blogs/michaelcalderone/1109/Layoffs_at_WaPo_.html, accessed Jan. 20, 2010.

28. "*HamptonRoads.tv* launches daily news webcast called *The Dot,*" online news release, Feb. 5, 2007; http://content.hamptonroads.com/story/cfm?story=118905&ran= 66573, accessed June 1, 2007.

29. Interview with Brian Clark by author, Jan. 21, 2010.

30. Kurt Andersen, "You Must Be Streaming," *New York*, Feb. 19, 2007, http://nymag.com/news/imperialcity/28152/, accessed Mar. 3, 2007.

31. "*Washingtonpost.com* Wins fourth Consecutive Edward R. Murrow," online news release, June 18, 2007; http://home.businesswire.com/portal/site/google/index.jsp?ndmViewId=news_view&news, accessed June 20, 2007.

32. "WHNPA Eyes of History 2007," White House News Photographers Association Web site on contest results; http://www.whnpa.org/contest/eyes2007/video/testresults/index.shtml0, accessed May 10, 2008.

33. Alex Hummel, "'Watching' your paper: Reporters, photographers take part in video, editing training," *The Northwestern*, Nov. 30, 2006; http://www.thenorthwestern.com/apps/pbcs.dll/article?AID=/20061130/OSH0101/61130, accessed Dec. 3, 2006.

34. Dirck Halstead, "The Coming Earthquake in Photography," *Digital Journalist*, Apr. 2007, digitaljournalist.org/issue0704/the-coming-earthquake-in-photography.html, accessed June 1, 2007.

35. George N. Gordon and Irving A. Falk, *TV Covers the Action*, Julian Messner, 1968, 126.

36. Ibid., 102.

37. Ibid., 116.

38. Mickey Osterreicher, "Putting Video Journalists in Perspective," *Shoptalk*, Sept. 12, 2007.

39. Michael Hoyt, "Jon Alpert: NBC's Odd Man Out," *Columbia Journalism Review*, Sept./Oct. 1991, http://backissues.cjrarchives.org/year91/5/alpert.asp, accessed June 15, 2004.

40. Ibid.

41. Ibid.

42. "VideoJournalists—Birth of a station," *ViewMagazine*, date unknown, http://www.viewmagazine.tv/videojos.html, accessed July 28, 2010.

43. Pat Aufderheide, "Vernacular Video," *Columbia Journalism Review*, Jan./Feb. 1995, http://backissues.cjrarchives.org/95/1/video.asp, accessed Jan. 17, 2008.

44. David Hinckley, "New York 1 celebrates its 15th anniversary," *New York Daily News*, Sept. 5, 2007, www.nydailynews.com/entertainment/tv/2007/09/05/2007–09–05_new_york_1_celebrates_its_15th_anniversa.html, accessed Sept. 6, 2007.

45. Halstead interview.

46. Ibid.

47. Evelyn Nussenbaum, "Cash-Strapped KRON Is Letting Advertisers Buy Into News Broadcasts," *San Francisco Chronicle*, Apr. 6, 2008, www.sfgate.com/c/a/2006/04/05/ddgbn120F41.dtl, accessed Jan. 14, 2009.

48. Michael Stoll, "Flagging Station Tries Reinventing TV News With Home-Video Tech, Grade The News," Dec. 21, 2005, www.gradethenews.org/2005/kron.htm, accessed Feb. 4, 2006.

49. Ibid.

50. Ibid.

51. NORCAL RTNDA, "VJ Revolution" panel discussion, Oct. 22, 2005.

52. Michael Malone, "Life Goes On at KRON," *Broadcasting & Cable*, Sept. 15, 2008, www.broadcastingcable.com/article/CA6595975.html, accessed Sept. 16, 2008. As of this writing Young Broadcasting still owns KRON.

53. Interview with Jonathan Bloom by KRON's Gary Radnich in 2006, www.youtub.com/watch?v=_v5YXldmh6c, accessed Mar. 8, 2008.

54. NORCAL RTNDA.

55. "WUSA to adopt one-person 'multimedia journalist' model for newsgathering," *Broadcast Engineering,* Dec. 19, 2008, http://broadcastengineering.com/news/WUSA-adopt-one-person-multimedia-journalist-model-newsgathering-1219/index.html, accessed Dec. 21, 2008.

56. Deborah Potter, "Star-Crossed Newsrooms," *American Journalism Review,* June/July 2008, www.ajr.org/article_printable.asp?id=4549, accessed Aug. 3, 2008.

57. "Paper shifts focus in digital world," *Detroit Free Press,* Dec. 17, 2008, www.freep.com/article/20081217/FREEPRESS/312170002, accessed Dec. 18, 2008.

58. Brian Stelter, "Can the Go-To Site Get You to Stay?" *New York Times,* Jan. 18, 2009, B2.

59. Mark Effron, "Broadcast Journalism Not Dead, Just Changing," *Television Week,* July 21, 2008, www.tvweek.com/news/2008/07/guest_commentary_broadcast_jou.php, accessed Oct. 29, 2008.

60. Diane Mermigas, "7 Reasons Why Broadcast Nets Need New Biz Models," *MediaPost,* Oct. 16, 2008, www.mediapost.com/publications/?fa=Articles.showArticleHomePage&art_aid=92758, accessed Oct. 20, 2008.

61. Sid Bedingfield, "The Problem with Broadcast News on the Web," *The Convergence Newsletter,* vol. 5, no. 7, Feb. 2008.

62. Joanne Ostrow, "As TV newsrooms shrink, reporters' roles expand," *Denver Post,* Dec. 16, 2008, www.denverpost.com/entertainment/ci_11239271, accessed Dec. 16, 2008.

63. ABC News-Mike Lee, July 28, 2001, http://abcnews.go.com/sections/wnt/WorldNewsTonight/LeeCam_notebook_feature.html, accessed June 4, 2004.

Chapter 1 Focus

1. Comments by Michael Rosenblum at "VJ Revolution," panel discussion at NORCAL RTNDA, Oct. 22, 2005.

2. Ibid.

3. Ibid.

4. Ibid.

5. Ibid.

6. Comments by Michael Rosenblum at "VJ in the Newsroom," panel at RTNDA, Apr. 26, 2006.

7. Ibid.

8. Ibid.

9. Ibid.

10. Comments from Michael Rosenblum at "The New VJs: Are They Just Another Way to Say 'One-Man Band' Or Are They the Future of Newsgathering?" panel at RTNDA, Apr. 17, 2007.

11. Ibid.

12. "VJ in the Newsroom."

13. Interview on C-SPAN, Nov. 20, 2008, http://www.solovj.com/audio-michael-rosenblum-on-c-span-qa, accessed Jan. 13, 2010.

14. Ibid.

15. Ibid.

16. Ibid.

Chapter 2

1. "VJ Revolution" panel at NORCAL RTNDA, Oct. 22, 2005.

2. Dale Schornack, "Back To The Future," blog on Feb. 5, 2008, www.news10.net/blog/schornack/schornack-blog.aspx, accessed Mar. 10, 2008.

3. Author's telephone interview with Matthew Zelkind, Jan. 14, 2009.

4. Dan Caesar, "KMOV joins trend, trims back in sports," *St. Louis Post-Dispatch,* June 21, 2008, www.stltoday.com/stltoday/sports/columnists.nsf/dancaesar/story/23A87F380C5686048625746F000C7909?OpenDocument, accessed June 23, 2008.

5. Kerry Sanders e-mail to author, June 15, 2004.

6. Poynter Institute Web site: https://www.communicationsmgr.com/projects/1296/solovideo.asp, accessed June 4, 2008.

7. Ibid.

8. Ibid.

9. Telephone interview with Deborah Potter by author, July 2, 2004.

10. Ibid.

11. Deborah Potter, "Point, Shoot and Ask: Does TV hurt coverage by using 'one-man bands?'" *American Journalism Review,* Apr. 2001, www.ajr.org/Article.asp?id=276, accessed June 1, 2004.

12. Audie Cornish, "All-in-One Reporters at Nashville Station," NPR, *All Things Considered,* Oct. 5, 2006, www.npr.org/template/story/story.php?storyid=6204241, accessed Oct. 19, 2006.

13. Response by David Page, Dec. 19, 2005, to Terry Heaton's blog "Enough is Enough!" Terry Heaton's PoMo Blog, Dec. 16, 2005, http://donatacom.com/archives/00001153.htm, accessed Feb. 10, 2007.

14. Nicole Lampa, "Keeping the journalism in videojournalism," Mar. 17, 2008, The Canadian Journalism Project, http://www.j-source.ca/english_new/detail.php?id=2256, accessed Jan. 13, 2010.

15. Paul Farhi, "WUSA Moves to One-Person News Crews," Dec. 12, 2008, *washingtonpost.com,* www.washingtonpost.com/wp-dyn/content/article/2008/12/11/AR2008121103976.html?sub=AR, accessed Dec. 12, 2008.

16. Natalie Bedell, "Newscaster Gary Reals Takes WUSA9 Buyout," *Falls Church News-Press,* Jan. 8, 2009, www.fcnp.com/index.php?option=com_content&view=article&id=3959:newscaster-gary-reals-takes-wusa9-buyout&catid=13:news-stories&itemid=76, accessed Jan. 11, 2009.

17. Eric Mansfield, "Me and Katie Couric . . . sort of . . . ," Sept. 23, 2008, http://eric-mansfield.blogspot.com, accessed Sept. 25, 2008.

18. Al Tompkins, "WTSP-TV Uses Skype to Broadcast Live Shot," *Al's Morning Meeting,* Jan. 7, 2009, www.poynter.org/column.asp?id=2&aid=156458, accessed Jan. 9, 2009.

19. John Strauss, "Print and Online: The Balancing Act," *Quill,* Mar. 2008, vol. 96, no. 2, 19.

20. Author's telephone interview with Dirck Halstead, June 19, 2008.

21. Ibid.

22. Harry Jaffe, "Reporters as Shooters—the Newest new Journalism Arrives at the Washington Post," *Washingtonian,* June 19, 2006, www.washingtonian.com/articles/people/2242.html, accessed June 20, 2006.

23. Letter from Stuart Watson to Shoptalk, Dec. 12, 2005.

24. Farhi, "WUSA Moves."

25. Sanders e-mail.

26. Melanie Woodrow, "Producing: The One-Man Band," *RTNDA Communicator,* Dec. 2006, vol. 60, no. 11, 44.

27. Interview with Richard Engel on *Telling the Truth, the Best in Broadcast Journalism,* Jan. 29, 2008, Thirteen/WNET and Columbia University Graduate School of Journalism.

28. Marisa Guthrie, "NBC's Richard Engel Wins Medill Medal of Courage," *Broadcasting and Cable,* Mar. 20, 2008, www.broadcastingcable.com/article/CA6543656.html?industryid=47181, accessed Mar. 21, 2008.

29. Society of Environmental Journalists Web site, www.sej.org/contest/index.htm, accessed Dec. 1, 2007.

30. Paula Hendrickson, "SEJ Finalist has Independent Streak," *Television Week,* Sept. 2, 2007, www.tvweek.com/news/2007/09/sej_finalist_has_independent.php, accessed Oct. 10, 2007.

31. Steve Krakauer, "So What Do You Do, Mara Schiavocampo, NBC Digital Journalist?" *MediaBistro,* Jan. 9, 2008, www.mediabistro.com/articles/cache/a10013.asp, accessed Nov. 1, 2008.

32. Andrea Rouda, "Talent, What it Takes to Have a Successful Reporter/Photographer Team," *RTNDA Communicator,* Sept. 2005, vol. 59, no. 8, 36.

33. Missouri School of Journalism alumni Web site, http://journalism.missouri.edu/alumni/jann-carl-82.html, accessed June 1, 2008.

34. Andy Douglas e-mails to author, June 16 and 17, 2004.

35. Bruce Cramer e-mail to author, June 22, 2004.

36. Brenda Madden Kimberlin e-mail to author, June 15, 2004.

37. Woodrow, "Producing."

38. Aaron Mermelstein e-mail to author, June 16, 2004.

39. Mike Sullivan e-mail to author, July 2, 2004.

40. Nancy Pasternak e-mail to author, June 15, 2004.

41. "VJ Revolution" panel.

42. Ibid.

43. Ibid.

44. Mary Angela Bock, "One Man Band: The Process and Product of Video Journalism" (Ph.D. dissertation, University of Pennsylvania, 2009), 223.

45. Author telephone interview with Wayne Freedman, July 26, 2010.

46. Ibid.

47. Tompkins, "WTSP-TV."

48. Krakauer, "So What."

49. Sandeep Junnarkar, "Q&A with Travis Fox, video journalist for *washington-post.com*," *Online Journalism Review,* Sept. 18, 2006, www.ojr.org/ojr/stories/600916Junnarkar/print.htm, accessed May 1, 2007.

50. Kathryn S. Wenner, "Snapshot of the Future," *American Journalism Review,* July/Aug. 2002, www.ajr.org/Article.asp?id=2592, accessed Oct. 29, 2008.

51. "Second Sight: A Video Essay by David Snider," *The Digital Filmmaker,* date unknown, http://www.dvnetwork.net/tdf/snider.html, accessed Jan. 19, 2009.

52. Ibid.

Chapter 3

1. Interview with Dan Weaver by author, Aug. 5, 2007.

2. Interview with Heidi McGuire by author, Aug. 4, 2007.

3. Al Tompkins, "WTSP-TV Uses Skype to Broadcast Live Shot," *Al's Morning Meeting,* Jan. 7, 2009, www.poynter.org/column.asp?id=2&aid=156458, accessed Jan. 9, 2009.

4. Interview with Brian Clark by author, July 10, 2007.

5. Interview with Dan Adams by author, Aug. 8, 2007.

6. E-mail interview with Travis Fox by Al Tompkins, "Best Practices: How Online Video Improves Journalism," *Al's Morning Meeting,* May 28, 2008, www.poynter.org/column.asp?id=2&aid=143996, accessed Oct. 27, 2008.

7. Clark interview.

8. Tracy Boyer, "Behind the Scenes of Honduras and the Hidden Hunger," Sept. 10, 2009, http://www.innovativeinteractivity.com/2009/09/10/behind-the-scenes-of-honduras-and-the-hidden-hunger/, accessed Jan. 2, 2010.

9. Ron Sylvester, "How one old reporting dog learned new multimedia tricks," *Quill,* Mar. 2008, vol. 96, no. 2, 13.

10. Jill Geisler, "What News Managers Owe Their Backpack Journalists," Mar. 9, 2009, www.poynter.org/column.asp?id=34&aid=159746, accessed Mar. 9, 2009.

Chapter 3 Focus

1. Based on interview by author with Brian Clark, July 9 and 10, 2007.

Chapter 4

1. Author's telephone interview with Dirck Halstead, June 19, 2008.

2. Al Tompkins, "WTSP-TV Uses Skype to Broadcast Live Shot," *Al's Morning Meeting,* Jan. 7, 2009, www.poynter.org/column.asp?id=2&aid=156458, accessed Jan. 9, 2009.

3. "Talk to the Newsroom: Editorial Director of Video," *New York Times,* May 17, 2009, http://www.nytimes.com/2009/05/18/business/media/18askthetimes.html?pagewanted=all, accessed Jan. 21, 2010.

4. Interview with Angela Grant by author, Jan. 17, 2010.

5. Charles Layton, "The Video Explosion," *American Journalism Review,* Dec./Jan. 2008, www.ajr.org/Article.asp?id=4428, accessed Jan. 30, 2008.

6. Interview with Marc Beaudin by author, Jan. 8, 2008.

7. Lucy Nicholson interview, "Kobre Guide to the Web's best videojournalism," http://kobreguide.com/content/howto/Lucy_Nicholson_Interview, accessed Jan. 13, 2010.

Chapter 4 Focus

1. Based on the author's research at WKRN, Apr. 2–4, 2007.

2. Penry left WKRN in 2010 to return to Kentucky.

Chapter 5

1. Interview with Ben de la Cruz by author, July 12, 2007.

2. Interview with Pierre Kattar by author, July 12, 2007.

3. Boyd Huppert, "Storytelling in the Moment," Poynter Institute Virtual Video Workshop, Sept. 19, 2009.

4. Author telephone interview with Wayne Freedman, July 26, 2010.

5. Bob Dotson, *Make it Memorable, Writing and Packaging TV News with Style*, 11, (Chicago: Bonus Books, 2000), 11–12.

6. "Talk to the Newsroom: Editorial Director of Video," *New York Times,* May 17, 2009, http://www.nytimes.com/2009/05/18/business/media/18askthetimes.html?page wanted=all, accessed Jan. 21, 2010.

7. Deborah Potter, "Natural sound stories: a how-to guide," NewsLab, Jan. 13, 2010, www.newslab.org/2010/01/13/natural-sound-stories-a-how-to-guide/, accessed Jan. 20, 2010.

8. Interview with Dan Weaver by author, Aug. 5, 2007.

9. Kyle Majors, "What is a Digital Correspondent," KGTV, http://www.10news.com/video/10215821/index.html, accessed May 8, 2008.

10. Ibid.

11. Unless otherwise noted, all quotes and information with Christina Pino-Marina are from an interview by the author, July 12, 2007.

12. Glen Canning, "BBC Video Journalist Tom Hepworth," YouTube video, http://www.videojournalist.ca/2009/12/09/bbc-video-journalist-tom-hepworth/, Dec. 9, 2009, accessed Jan. 6, 2010.

13. Glenn Hartong, "Conveying a tragic scene is difficult, but necessary," *Cincinnati Enquirer,* Apr. 5, 2008, http://news.enquirer.com/apps/pbcs.dll/article?AID=/20080405/NEWS01/804050362/-1/colerain, accessed Apr. 20, 2008.

14. Melanie Woodrow, "Producing: The One-Man Band," *RTNDA Communicator,* Dec. 2006, vol. 60, no. 11, 44.

15. Weaver interview.

16. Lynn French, "Lessons from a Backpack Journalist," *Al's Morning Meeting,* June 25, 2008, www.poynter.org/column.asp?id=2, accessed June 29, 2008.

17. Interview with Dan Adams by author, Aug. 8, 2007.

18. Interview with Brian Clark by author, July 10, 2007.

19. Becky Blanton, "Great tips," response to Lynn French on *Al's Morning Meeting,* June 25, 2008, www.poynter.org/article_feedback/article_feedback_list.asp?user=&id=144839, accessed Aug. 24, 2008.

Chapter 5 Focus

1. Based on author's research at KUSA, Aug. 4, 2007.

Chapter 6

1. "The Five Shot Rule," BBC online training video, http://www.bbctraining.com/modules/5915/video/1.2.2.htm, accessed Jan. 13, 2010.
2. Interview with Dan Adams by author, Aug. 8, 2007.
3. Interview with Brian Clark by author, July 10, 2007.
4. Interview with Jesse Vega by author, Jan. 7, 2008.
5. Darren Durlach, "Six Essential Skills to Maximize Your Storytelling Process," Poynter Institute Virtual Video Workshop, Sept. 19, 2009.
6. Response to "Web video-tips from BBC.com," Sept. 4, 2008, http://video2zero.com/web-video-tips-from-bbccom/, accessed Jan. 13, 2010.
7. Paula Hendrickson, "SEJ Finalist has Independent Streak," *Television Week,* Sept. 2, 2007, www.tvweek.com/news/2007/09/sej_finalist_has_independent.php, accessed Sept. 5, 2007.

Chapter 6 Focus

1. Cliff Etzel, "Equipment," www.solovj.com/equipment, accessed Jan. 22, 2010.
2. Edward J. Delaney, "Profile of a backpacker: Inside Mara Schiavocampo's toolkit," Nieman Journalism Lab, Jan. 12, 2009, http://www.niemanlab.org/2009/01/mara-schi-avocampo-backpack-journalist/, accessed Jan. 22, 2010.
3. James Careless, "Going Solo, Backpack journalism may not be new, but new technologies—and harsh financial truths—have made it more useful to newsrooms than ever," *RTNDA Communicator,* May 18, 2009, www.rtnda.org/pages/posts/going-solo509.php, accessed May 24, 2009.
4. Ibid.
5. Etzel, "Equipment."
6. Delaney, "Profile."

Chapter 7

1. Scott Atkinson, "VJ Pros and Cons," no date, NewsLab, www.newslab.org/articles/vjs2.htm accessed June 20, 2008.
2. Abe Rosenberg, "Before You Write a Word," *RTNDA Communicator,* Dec. 1998, 55.
3. Comments by the News 12 Long Island reporter at "TV News Storytelling" panel at Society of Professional Journalists regional conference, Apr. 4, 2007, Hempstead, New York.
4. Boyd Huppert, "Storytelling in the Moment," Poynter Institute, Virtual Video Workshop, Sept. 19, 2009.
5. Interview with Dan Weaver by author, Aug. 5, 2007.
6. "TV News Storytelling" panel.

7. Huppert, "Storytelling."

8. Deborah Potter and Annie Lang, "Making Stories Memorable," NewsLab, no date, www.newslab.org/research/makingmemorable.htm, accessed Apr. 3, 2008.

9. "How Viewers View the News," NewsLab, no date, http:www.newslab.org/research/howview.htm, accessed Apr. 3, 2008.

10. Interview with Patti Dennis by author, Aug. 3, 2007.

11. The author has no citation for this story, which ran on NBC's closed-circuit feed to NBC News Channel affiliates in the spring of 1995.

Chapter 8

1. Dave Cupp and Ann Utterback, "Broadcast narration for new platforms," News-Lab, Aug. 21, 2009, www.newslab.org/2009/08/21/broadcast-narration-for-new-platforms/, accessed Jan. 20, 2010.

2. Al Thompson, "How to Improve Your Voice (Even if You Hate Your Voice)," *Al's Morning Meeting*, July 5, 2007, www.poynter.org/column.asp?id=2&aid=126101, accessed Nov. 10, 2007.

3. Interview with Jerry Barlar by author, Apr. 2, 2007.

4. Colin Mulvany, "What we can learn from TV news shooters," Jan. 5, 2008, http:masteringmultimedia.wordpress.com/2008/01/05/what-we-can-learn-from-tv-news-shooters/, accessed Mar. 1, 2008.

5. Author telephone interview with Wayne Freedman, July 26, 2010.

6. Interview with Ben de la Cruz by author, July 12, 2007.

7. "How Viewers View the News," NewsLab, no date, http:www.newslab.org/research/howview.htm, accessed Apr. 3, 2008.

8. Greg T. Johnson, "Seven Habits of Highly Effective Editing," Poynter Institute Virtual Video Workshop, Sept. 19, 2009.

9. The RTDNA Code of Ethics and Professional Conduct can be found at http://www.rtdna.org/pages/media_items/code-of-ethics-and-professional-conduct48.php?id=48.

10. Johnson, "Seven Habits."

11. Pierre Kattar, "Let's Dance: Finding the Right Voice and Approach for Your Stories," Poynter Institute, Virtual Video Workshop, Sept. 19, 2009.

12. Ibid.

13. "Talk to the Newsroom: Editorial Director of Video," *New York Times,* May 17, 2009, http://www.nytimes.com/2009/05/18/business/media/18askthetimes.html?pagewanted=all, accessed Jan. 21, 2010.

14. Richard Koci Hernandez, "Multimedia Rules to Live By and Seven Steps to Training Yourself," www.multimediashooter.com/wp/tutorials/multimedia-rules-to-live-by-and-seven-steps-to-training-yourself, Dec. 24, 2009, accessed Dec. 28, 2009.

15. Kattar, "Let's Dance."

16. "Talk to the Newsroom."

17. Gabriel Dance, "Interactive Narratives," News21 Spring Training 2010, Feb. 2010, http://news21.com/st022010/, accessed Aug. 15, 2010.

18. Author interview with Roger M. Richards, July 10, 2007.

Chapter 8 Focus

1. See Joe Little's standups on YouTube at:
http://www.youtube.com/watch?v=TO356cp9tKE&eurl=http://www.b-roll.net/forum/showthread.php?t=22796.

2. Author interview with Heidi McGuire, Aug. 5, 2007.

3. Glen Canning, "BBC Video Journalist Tom Hepworth," YouTube video, Dec. 9, 2009, http://www.videojournalist.ca/2009/12/09/bbc-video-journalist-tom-hepworth/, accessed Jan. 6, 2010.

Chapter 9

1. "Talk to the Newsroom: Editorial Director of Video," *New York Times,* May 17, 2009, http://www.nytimes.com/2009/05/18/business/media/18askthetimes.html?pagewanted=all, accessed Jan. 21, 2010.

2. Unless otherwise noted, quotes and information with Chet Rhodes are from an interview by the author on July 13, 2007.

3. "The New VJs: Are They Just Another Way to Say 'One-Man Band' Or Are They the Future of Newsgathering?" panel discussion at RTNDA convention, Apr. 17, 2007.

4. Michael Calderone, "WaPo cuts several positions," *POLITICO,* Nov. 20, 2009, www.politico.com/blogs/michaelcalderone/1109/Layoffs_at_WaPo_.html, accessed Jan. 20, 2010.

5. Sandeep Junnarkar, "Q&A with Travis Fox, video journalist for *washingtonpost.com,*" *Online Journalism Review,* Sept. 18, 2006, www.ojr.org/ojr/stories/600916Junnarkar/print.htm, accessed Mar. 10, 2007.

6. Clint Brewer, "The New Darwinism," *Quill,* Mar. 2008, vol. 96, no. 2, 3.

7. "Research finds professional video is tops on the Web," *Boston Business Journal,* Jan. 21, 2008, http://boston.bizjournals.com/boston/stories/2008/01/21/daily4.html, accessed Jan. 28, 2008.

8. Kurt Andersen, "You Must Be Streaming," *New York,* Feb. 19, 2007, http://nymag.com/news/imperialcity/28152/, accessed Mar. 3, 2007.

9. Allison J. Waldmann, "*Newsweek.com* Seeds Site With Video," *The Ad Age,* Nov. 12, 2007, http://adage.com/webvideoreport/article?article_id=128347, accessed Nov. 12, 2007.

10. Letter to *Shoptalk* from Doug Caldwell, Aug. 21, 2007.

11. "C-J Hires a Videographer," *Ville Voice,* Aug. 13, 2007, www:thevillevoice.com/2007/08/, accessed Aug. 28, 2007.

12. *Shoptalk,* Aug. 17, 2007.

13. Emma Heald, "US: Newspapers competing with broadcast for TV awards," Dec. 16, 2008, www.editorsweblog.org/multimedia/2008/12/us_newspapers_competing_with_broadcast_f.php, accessed Dec. 16, 2008.

14. Interview with Kate Marymont by author, Jan. 7, 2008.

15. Phone interview with Kate Marymont by author, Dec. 5, 2007.

16. Marymont interview, Jan. 7, 2008.

17. Interview with Cindy McCurry-Ross by author, Jan. 7, 2008.

18. Interview with Dave Breitenstein by author, Jan. 8, 2008.

19. Joe Strupp, "Special Report: Going Mobile—The End of the Newsroom As We Know It?" *Editor & Publisher,* May 21, 2008, http://www.editorandpublisher.com/eandp/news/article_display.jsp?vnu_content_id=1003805733, accessed June 8, 2008.

20. Ibid.

21. Ibid.

22. "How Not To Do Newspaper Video," *The Digital Journalist,* May 2008, accessed June 19, 2008, www.digitaljournalist.org/issue0805/how-not-to-do-newspaper-video.html, accessed June 20, 2008.

23. *NBC Nightly News* senior broadcast producer Bob Epstein e-mail to author, June 6, 2008.

24. "Prison Puppies," *NBC Nightly News,* June 2, 2008 and the *New York Times,* June 1, 2008, http://video.on.nytimes.com/, accessed June 2, 2008.

25. "At NYC Meeting: Top Media Companies Vow Online Explosion," *Editor and Publisher,* Dec. 5, 2007, www.editorandpublisher.com/eandp/news/article_display.jsp?vnu_content_id=1003681421, accessed Dec. 6, 2007.

26. Interview with Tom Kennedy by author, July 12, 2007.

27. Unless otherwise noted, all quotes and information with Christina Pino-Marina are from an interview by the author, July 12, 2007.

28. Telephone interview with Christina Pino-Marina by author, Jan. 19, 2010. Besides raising a family, she also is teaching videojournalism as an adjunct professor.

29. Christina Pino-Marina, "Behind the Lens, Who We Are," a bio on the *washingtonpost.com* Web site, blog.washingtonpost.com/behind-the-lens/2006/12/who_we_are.html, accessed Aug. 28, 2007.

30. "Talk to the Newsroom."

31. All quotes and information about Ben de la Cruz are from an interview by the author, July 12, 2007.

32. Ju-Don Roberts, "Welcome to Behind the Lens," Dec. 15, 2006, blog.*washingtonpost.com*/behind-the-lens/documentary-video/, accessed May 3, 2007.

33. Al Tompkins, "Tuesday Edition: 2007 Best of Television Photojournalism Contest," Mar. 5, 2007, www.poynter.org/content/content_print.asp?id=119369, accessed Apr. 16, 2007.

34. Ibid.

35. Ibid.

Chapter 9 Focus

1. Quotes and information about Dirck Halstead from a telephone interview with Halstead by author, June 19, 2008.

2. Http://rogermrichards.com, accessed Jan. 15, 2010.

3. Quotes and information about Roger Richards from an interview with Richards by author, July 10, 2007.

4. You can read more about Platypus on Dirck Halstead's blog: http://www.prague-workshops.com/blogs/dhalstead.

Chapter 10

1. Based on author's research visit to WKRN, Apr. 2–4, 2007.

2. Sabato was let go from the news director's position by WKRN a month later.

3. Based on author's research visit to Houston, Jan. 17, 2010. Angela Grant moved to Austin, Texas, in March 2010 to pursue freelance multimedia journalism work.

4. You can view this story at http://instantnewswestu.com/2010/01/17/7509/ or on YouTube at http://www.youtube.com/watch?v=NoOqyLqiLfU.

5. Based on author's research visit to KUSA, Aug. 5, 2007.

6. Based on author's research visit to *Fort Myers News-Press,* Jan. 7–8, 2008.

7. Christine Lee e-mail to author, Feb. 21, 2008.

8. Christine Lee e-mail to author, Mar. 5, 2008.

9. From Christine Lee's Web site, http://sites.google.com/site/uclasian/home, accessed Jan. 12, 2010.

10. Christine Lee e-mail to author Jan. 15, 2010.

Chapter 10 Focus

1. Deborah Potter, "Time-savers for solo journalists," NewsLab, July 14, 2010, http://www.newslab.org/2010/07/14/time-savers-for-solo-journalists/, accessed July 20, 2010.

Chapter 11

1. An expansion of work first published by the author as "Story Bored," *RTNDA Communicator,* Dec. 2002, vol. 56, no. 11.

2. Al Tompkins, "CNN Show Written, Edited, Produced by Photojournalists," *Al's Morning Meeting,* Jan. 5, 2009, www.poynter.org/column.asp?id=2&aid=156257, accessed Jan. 7, 2009.

3. Robert A. Papper, *Broadcast News & Writing Stylebook,* 3rd ed. (Boston: Allyn and Bacon, 2005), 137.

4. Robert Niles, "Keeping your job in journalism," *Online Journalism Review,* www.ojr.org/ojr/stories/080305niles, accessed June 30, 2008.

5. Deborah Potter, "A view from the future," NewsLab, Dec. 21, 2009, www.newslab.org/2009/12/21/a-view-from-the-future/, accessed Jan. 20, 2010.

6. 2009 Annual Survey of Journalism & Mass Communication Graduates, Grady College of Journalism and Mass Communication, University of Georgia, Aug. 4, 2010, http://www.grady.uga.edu/annualsurveys/Graduate_Survey/Graduate_2009/Grad2009MergedB&W.pdf, accessed Aug. 4, 2010. See Chart 22, page 39 for details.

7. http://huffpostfund.org/multimedia, accessed Jan. 13, 2010.

8. Roy Greenslade, "Hadfield quits Telegraph group, saying newspapers have no future," *Guardian,* Jan. 15, 2010, http://www.guardian.co.uk/media/greenslade/2010/jan/15/telegraphmediagroup-willlewis, accessed Jan. 20, 2010.

9. "Amy Gahran on the Future Journalist," online video interview on *OurBlook,* date unknown. http://www.ourblook.com/Future-Journalist/Amy-Gahran-on-the-Future-Journalist.html, accessed July 29, 2010.

10. Chris Albrecht, "Get Ready for 'OmniVideo,'" *New TeeVee,* June 22, 2008, http://newteevee.com/2008/06/22/get-ready-for-omnivideo/#more-4421, accessed June 23, 2008.

11. "Be a mobile phone journalist," *ViewMagazine.tv,* http://www.viewmagazine.tv/Beamobilephonereporter.php, accessed Jan. 13, 2010.

12. Gio Benitez, "How good is the iPhone's new video camera?" WFOR, June 22, 2009, http://cbs4.com/local/iphone.Apple.Gio.2.1054634.html, accessed June 23, 2009.

13. Al Tompkins, "WTSP-TV Uses Skype to Broadcast Live Shot," *Al's Morning Meeting,* Jan. 7, 2009, www.poynter.org/column.asp?id=2&aid=156458, accessed Jan. 9, 2009.

14. Lynn French, "Lessons from a Backpack Journalist," *Al's Morning Meeting,* June 25, 2008, www.poynter.org/column.asp?id=2, accessed June 25, 2008.

15. Paula Hendrickson, "SEJ Finalist has Independent Streak," *Television Week,* Sept. 2, 2007, www.tvweek.com/news/2007/09/sej_finalist_has_independent.php, accessed Oct. 10, 2008.

16. Ibid.

17. Terry Heaton, "A Reasonable View of Tomorrow," Apr. 25, 2008, http://www.the-pomoblog.com/papers/pomo80.htm, accessed May 5, 2008.

18. Howard Kurtz, "Media Web Site Pushes Entrepreneurial Model," *Washington Post,* June 8, 2009, www.washingtonpost.com/wp-dyn/content/linkset/2005/04/11/LI2005041100587.html, accessed June 9, 2009.

19. Ibid.

20. Video on Travel Academy Web site, www.travelchannel.com/Academy/Big_Picture, accessed May 10, 2008.

21. Ken Kobré, "The Future of Videojournalism: Stay ahead of the curve by following these trends," *Digital Journalist,* Apr. 2009, http://www.digitaljournalist.org/issue0904/the-future-of-videojournalism.html, accessed Jan. 13, 2010.

22. Daniel Axelrod, "Digitize your job prospects," *Quill,* May/June 2010, vol. 98, no. 3, 25.

23. *OurBlook,* "Amy Gahran."

24. Missouri School of Journalism alumni Web site, http://journalism.missouri.edu/alumni/elizabeth-vargas-84.html, accessed May 5, 2008.

Chapter 11 Focus

1. Tompkins ended publication of *Al's Morning Meeting,* in October, 2010. Al Tompkins, "Goodbye Al's Morning Meeting, Hello Something New," Oct. 4, 2010, http://www.poynter.org/latest-news/als-morning-meeting/106088/goodbye-als-morning-meeting-hello-something-new/, accessed March 1, 2011.

2. E-mail interview of Al Tompkins by author, Jan. 7, 2010.

Index

About the Author

G. Stuart Smith is Associate Professor in the Department of Journalism, Media Studies, and Public Relations at Hofstra University. He has produced two documentaries, working mostly as a solo videojournalist, and has won over two dozen awards for his work as a videojournalist and documentary filmmaker. He resides in Freeport, New York.